Finding a Treasure

101 Devotions
For Parents of Special Children

BY TRACY BRELAND

Presented To

_____

ON

_____

BY

_____

Finding a Treasure

101 Devotions
For Parents of
Special Children

BY TRACY BRELAND

All Scripture is from The New King James Version (NKJV) unless otherwise noted.

Scripture quotations marked (NKJV) are taken from The New King James Version. Copyright © 1979, 1980, 1982, Thomas Nelson, Inc.

Scripture quotations marked (KJV) are taken from The King James Version. Copyright © 1979, 1980, 1982, Thomas Nelson, Inc.

Scripture quotations marked (NIV) are taken from The Holy Bible: New International Version® NIV ®. Copyright © 1973, 1978, 1984 by International Bible Society. Used by permission of Zondervan Publishing House. All rights reserved.

Scripture taken from The Message. Copyright 1993, 1994, 1995, 1996, 2000, 2001, 2002. Used by permission of NavPress Publishing Group.

Scripture quotations marked (NAS) are taken from the New American Standard Bible. Copyright © the Lockman Foundation 1960, 1962, 1963, 1968, 1971, 1972, 1973, 1975, 1977. Used by permission.

Verses marked (TLB) are taken from The Living Bible © 1971. Used by permission of Tyndale House Publishers, Inc., Wheaton, IL. All rights reserved.

Scripture taken from the Good News Translation in Today's English Version— Second Edition Copyright © 1992 by American Bible Society. Used by permission.

Scripture quotations marked (NLT) are taken from the Holy Bible, New Living Translation, copyright 1996, 2004. Used by permission of Tyndale House Publishers, Inc., Wheaton, IL. All rights reserved.

Author photography by www.MelissaKeyGallery.com.

978-0-9840673-0-5
Finding a Treasure
101 Devotions for Parents of Special Children

Published by Mountz Media & Publishing
P.O. Box 702398
Tulsa, Oklahoma 74170-2398
918-296-0995
www.mountzmedia.com

Printed in the United States of America. All rights reserved under International Copyright Law. Contents and/or cover may not be reproduced in whole or in part in any form without the express written consent of the publisher.

What People Are Saying:

Pastor Billy Joe Daugherty, Victory Christian Center: "Every child is special, especially yours. Each one is valuable and precious. Tracy and her husband have raised five beautiful children in the ways of the Lord. What Tracy has written is powerful! The truth of the scripture is proclaimed with clarity and with deep insight. The personal illustrations and reflection on the details of their experiences will make you laugh, cry, relax and jump up with a shout. You will definitely be in better position to put the Word of God into practice in your daily life. Our children are God's special treasure to us."

Mark Harris, multiple Dove Award winner and Grammy-nominated singer and songwriter: "I have known John and Tracy Breland for over 20 years, and the Brelands have one of the most Christ-centered homes in America. I have literally watched them raise Caroline, their special needs child, with grace filled with love. They truly have shown the joy that can be found through such a treasure in their home. This book is a wonderful gift first to anyone who is blessed with a special needs child and everyone else wanting daily doses of inspiration from the heart of a mother."

Marcia Mitchell, Founder and CEO, The Little Light House: "Tracy Breland has created jewels of encouragement and hope in the pages of her book *Finding a Treasure*. Each devotional evolves out of the Word of God and reflects precious insights and principles which have been etched in the lives of Tracy and her beautiful family. Her transparency allows the reader to relate to the real life experiences she so poignantly shares. Throughout the pages, she points to perfect peace and victory found in a personal relationship with Christ. Parents who have been blessed with a child with special needs will truly find a "treasure" in this inspirational piece."

Contents

INTRODUCTION 1
ONE — NEITHER 7
TWO — ROY AND DALE 9
THREE — THE HEART 11
FOUR — HIGH PLACES 13
FIVE — EVER INCREASING 15
SIX — KINDNESS 17
SEVEN — SPEAK LIFE 19
EIGHT — JOY WILL COME 21
NINE — FALL IN LOVE 23
TEN — YOUR REDEEMER IS ALIVE 25
ELEVEN — DO NOT WORRY 27
TWELVE — NOTHING IS IMPOSSIBLE 29
THIRTEEN — A FIRM FOUNDATION 31
FOURTEEN — WALK BY FAITH 33
FIFTEEN — WAIT EAGERLY 35
SIXTEEN — THE FIGHT OF FAITH 37
SEVENTEEN — TRUTH VERSUS LIES 39
EIGHTEEN — GOD MEANT IT FOR GOOD 41
NINETEEN — HOW TO RECEIVE YOUR INHERITANCE 43
TWENTY — ENDURANCE 45
TWENTY-ONE — HOLD FAST 47
TWENTY-TWO — FINDING A TREASURE 49
TWENTY-THREE — BELIEVING ISN'T PRETENDING 51
TWENTY-FOUR — A NEW KIND OF FAST 53
TWENTY-FIVE — I WILL 55
TWENTY-SIX — PERFECT LOVE 57
TWENTY-SEVEN — BREAKFAST OF CHAMPIONS 59

~I~

Twenty-eight — Come and Worship	61
Twenty-nine — The Next Level	63
Thirty — Prophecy Comes to Pass	65
Thirty-one — What Kind of Women	67
Thirty-two — All Things	69
Thirty-three — Wait for the Perfect Timing	71
Thirty-four — Set Free!	73
Thirty-five — Great Peace	75
Thirty-six — Follow the Leader	77
Thirty-seven — Get Over to the Other Side	79
Thirty-eight — Midnight Hour	81
Thirty-nine — Who's Listening?	83
Forty — Dig Deep	85
Forty-one — A Prophet	87
Forty-two — Family Now	89
Forty-three — Hard Pressed	91
Forty-four — Take a Walk	93
Forty-five — Disbelief	95
Forty-six — Strong in Spirit	97
Forty-seven — State Your Case	99
Forty-eight — Let It Go	101
Forty-nine — Pass the Test	103
Fifty — Surpassing Peace	105
Fifty-one — Follow Him	107
Fifty-two — Power	109
Fifty-three — Diagnosed	111
Fifty-four — Touch Him	113
Fifty-five — A Strong Consolation	115
Fifty-six — A Perfect Way	117
Fifty-seven — Get Filled Up	119
Fifty-eight — A Virtuous Mother	121
Fifty-nine — Broken Hearted	123
Sixty — Never Forsaken	125
Sixty-one — Perfect	127
Sixty-two — Family	129

SIXTY-THREE — BEFORE I GO TO BED 131
SIXTY-FOUR — PARTAKE 133
SIXTY-FIVE — EARLY MORNING PRAYER 135
SIXTY-SIX — OUR RESCUER. 137
SIXTY-SEVEN — BOASTING 139
SIXTY-EIGHT — THE PRODIGAL SON 141
SIXTY-NINE — THIS LITTLE LIGHT OF MINE. 143
SEVENTY — THE LION, THE BEAR, OH NO 145
SEVENTY-ONE — EBENEZER 147
SEVENTY-TWO — PERFUME 149
SEVENTY-THREE — RAISING CHILDREN. 151
SEVENTY-FOUR — DAILY BREAD 153
SEVENTY-FIVE — PASS IT ON. 155
SEVENTY-SIX — TURN, TURN FROM SIN AND SORROW . . 157
SEVENTY-SEVEN — OH, BE CAREFUL LITTLE EARS
    WHAT YOU HEAR 159
SEVENTY-EIGHT — THE CONTENT OF THE HEART. 161
SEVENTY-NINE — TO ALL GENERATIONS 163
EIGHTY — FORGET ABOUT YOURSELF 165
EIGHTY-ONE — THIRSTY? 167
EIGHTY-TWO — FOREVER FRIENDS 169
EIGHTY-THREE — AFRAID OF THE DARK 171
EIGHTY-FOUR — HAPPILY EVER AFTER 173
EIGHTY-FIVE — FEAR NOT 175
EIGHTY-SIX — FOLLOW. 177
EIGHTY-SEVEN — ANCHORS AWAY. 179
EIGHTY-EIGHT — KEEP PADDLING. 181
EIGHTY-NINE — THE WORD CAUSES US TO GROW. 183
NINETY — A HELPING HAND 185
NINETY-ONE — 'MAMA'. 187
NINETY-TWO — HE DIRECTS 189
NINETY-THREE — EXAMINE 191
NINETY-FOUR — START EARLY 193
NINETY-FIVE — WRITE IT DOWN 195
NINETY-SIX — WISH OR WORK 197

~III~

Ninety-seven — Friction 199
Ninety-eight — See 201
Ninety-nine — Mountain or Mole Hill 203
One hundred — The Great Exchange 205
One hundred and one — It Is Finished 207

Introduction

Growing up in a large family, my dream was to someday have a large family of my own. Before long I met and married the man of my dreams and shared with him my dream of having at least 10 children. Needless to say, he was quite shocked, but the idea soon grew on him. In fact, a little over a year into our marriage I became pregnant, and like many of you, I was overjoyed with the news. I was teaching school in Alabama at the time, and all of life was perfect.

However, things were about to change. A few months into the pregnancy, I experienced complications and ended up losing my first baby. It felt as though the world grew dark. With great expectation I tried again and again, but experienced another miscarriage. My heart was breaking, and my dream of a large family seemed far off.

Yet, many times it's darkest right before the dawn. I finally conceived and gave birth to my first child, Elizabeth Rose. I truly was the happiest woman alive. My daughter never left my side; I was in complete bliss being a mother. When my precious little one was about two, I became pregnant again.

With my previous experience, I was a little apprehensive, but really excited too. Everything seemed to be going along smoothly until I went for my first ultrasound. Doctors thought they saw something unusual in the baby's kidneys, and they sent me for further testing. I literally was terrified. We were thankful that all of the tests came back normal, and I continued to plan for the arrival of my second child.

The due date came and went, and my unborn baby, Caroline, wasn't ready to meet the world yet. I didn't really blame her. By May 21, 1995 I was awake all night with pains, so early that morning I decided to go to the hospital. The nurses explained that things were progressing, but it wasn't time yet. So I was given a room and began to wait. I was delivering naturally, and around noon the pains seemed unbearable. Still, the nurses were not convinced that it was time to call the doctor. So I went over their heads and asked the real authority—my mother. She instructed me to go ahead and begin labor, and she was right. The baby almost arrived before the doctor.

The birthing process went quickly, and little Caroline burst on the scene weighing in at 10 pounds and 2 ounces. I had carried her about two weeks over the due date so she was good and healthy—and *big!* So very relieved that the worst was over, I now had two little girls. That was a big deal to me because I never had a sister.

It wasn't long before nurses took my new baby away to start giving her oxygen, but they assured me that she was all right. I was so completely exhausted from the long and natural birth, I decided to trust them and not be my usual nosey self.

Then in the middle of the night, one nurse rocked my world. She entered my hospital room to take my vitals, but in the most unprofessional way possible, she began spilling out what the doctors were thinking—all kinds of negative comments and speculations about *my* baby. I was shocked. Speechless. Stunned.

I was so focused on her words that I thought I was alone until later my husband reminded me that he was actually there with me. I felt as if I were looking through a tunnel, and this nurse was the only one in the world talking. I felt like I was in a dream—a nightmare.

We were too overcome to respond to her with even a single word, but she continued talking. She went on to tell us about an uncle she had who was mentally challenged, but quite frankly, she didn't use nice words at all. Her words painted an awful picture full of heartache and negativity. And when she left the room, we were left devastated.

The next morning the staff brought in my new Caroline, and I dressed her in pink and wrapped her up tightly. I completely erased from my mind the visit from the nurse that seemed like a nightmare. I erased all medical suspicions from my mind and fell head over heels in love with my dark-haired little girl. Doctors insisted on doing some tests before we left the hospital, but I had strong doubts about it all. After all, I didn't see a thing wrong with my child. When I looked at her, I saw perfection.

A week later I returned to the doctor's office for her one-week checkup, and I was more convinced than ever that she was fine. I walked into the doctor's office feeling pretty good. Unfortunately, our regular pediatrician was not in the office so we'd been scheduled with another doctor instead.

In that little exam room, this other doctor took every dream I ever had and ripped them to shreds. She started out by confirming that, in fact, Caroline was officially diagnosed with Down syndrome. The doctor didn't stop there. She continued saying that all my miscarriages were probably a result of something being wrong with the other babies as well. Her final blow was an official admonition not to have any more children.

I felt like I'd been punched in the stomach. I was in shock. I felt numb.

I don't remember much more than leaving as fast as I could with my two little girls—one I held very tightly. As I walked across the parking lot, I had the strongest urge to take my baby and run. I knew I loved little Caroline unconditionally, but I didn't trust the world.

The days and months that followed were some of the darkest times in my life. I couldn't taste food for months. I couldn't sing. I didn't know whether to be mad at the world—or mad at myself. Mostly, I couldn't escape the guilt deep down inside that I had somehow caused this life-altering trauma.

To make matters even more complex, we were living in Alabama at the time – away from all friends and family. I just about lost all hope. But thank God, He doesn't let the world crush us.

Up to that time in my life, I'd never used any birth control measures because I had experienced a hard enough time getting pregnant. But at this point, the doctor prescribed birth control because, of course, all the medical professionals were sure I wouldn't want any more children. Nevertheless, even in my depression I was still kind of spunky. The first morning I was given the birth control pills, I got a little angry and tired of people telling me what to do. I thought, *Am I going to let these people control my life or am I going to let God control my life?*

So I tossed the pills way back in the cabinet and decided right then and there that I would walk by faith. I also thought it would be a long time before I'd get pregnant again anyway. Wrong. To my surprise—and everyone else's—I found out I was pregnant again when Caroline was only four months old. Waves of utter joy came along only to be knocked down by waves of utter fear.

Three months into the pregnancy, I went for an ultrasound, which was scary for me in light of my recent history. I kept trying to explain to the doctor that I seemed very big for only three months along, but he felt it was because I had just given birth five months earlier. It's unbelievable really, isn't it?

As I laid down on the table, the doctor began the ultrasound process. The first thing I said was, "Well, I hope the baby is OK!"

She waited a while and then replied, "They look great!"

"*They?!*" I said, startled.

"You didn't know you were having twins?" she asked.

No. I didn't know.

And my husband, John, who was holding five-month-old Caroline almost passed out.

The news was still sinking in, but clearly we were completely elated with joy! I still remember that day like it was yesterday. It was December 19, 1995, and I felt my heart began to heal. John and I lay down in bed that night and whispered thanks to God—only He could have done this. Only He could bless us this way.

The twins were due in May, one year after Caroline had been born. Actually, the twins came early—our delivery came quickly.

At different times throughout the pregnancy, I was tortured with fear-filled thoughts, and I had to fight a feeling of ignorance about having more children. I was even approached by a few people who couldn't believe John and I would allow ourselves to have another child. But on April 19, we had two healthy babies, a boy and a girl. We named them John and Anna.

While the twins were not even two years old, the Lord blessed us with another son, David, who is the baby of the family. Now we're five in all. And though we're not the 10 I originally desired, through all the laughter and tears—and ups and downs—I wouldn't change a thing. The Lord has worked in my life to help me see the good and the joy in everything.

I hope I never forget when Dale Evans, who also had a baby with Down syndrome, grabbed my hand one day and said, "All things work together for the good of those who love God and are called according to His purpose." So from that moment to this, I came to believe that what the devil meant for bad God would turn around for His good. My whole outlook on life changed through the power of God's Word.

The testimonies of truth that I share in this book are the very truths that set me free to enjoy the life that God gave my family and me. I hope to comfort you with the same comfort God gave me.

I now teach third grade, and I'm pioneering a special education program at our school. Our five children are all active, which keeps John and I active. Caroline—*my special treasure*—goes to school and takes piano lessons and plays basketball. She is caught often saying "I love my life!" and isn't that what every parent wants to hear?

ONE

Neither

NOW AS JESUS PASSED BY, HE SAW A MAN WHO WAS BLIND FROM BIRTH. AND HIS DISCIPLES ASKED HIM, SAYING "RABBI, WHO SINNED, THIS MAN OR HIS PARENTS THAT HE WAS BORN BLIND?" JESUS ANSWERED, "NEITHER THIS MAN NOR HIS PARENTS, BUT THAT THE WORKS OF GOD MIGHT BE REVEALED IN HIM." —JOHN 9:1-3

Never be afraid to ask questions. After all, this question from the disciples set me free!

The idea of having a child with any complications was overwhelming enough, but it was followed by waves of guilt. I knew my past, and I knew I wasn't perfect so I quickly took the blame. Blame and guilt are from the devil, but he loves to heap these on people when they're going through difficult times. I was really convinced without a doubt that I was to blame for my baby Caroline's diagnosis of Down syndrome.

When it came down to it, I felt like a lesser person to begin with so it wasn't difficult to believe this had happened to me instead of all the great people I knew. I felt this was payment for all the sins I'd ever committed. This guilt and blame increased until I was thoroughly convinced that I was to pay for all my sins.

Yet, one day the Lord brought this Scripture before my eyes: "You shall know the truth and the truth will make you free" (John 8:32). I started searching God's Word and asking Him what He thought. Thank God, He began to answer me.

I will never forget the day I came across this Scripture in John 9 where the disciples were questioning who had caused the man to be born blind—he or his parents. Jesus blew them all away with one word. Jesus said, *"Neither!"*

Praise God! The chains of guilt that had held me captive for years fell off instantly in a moment of truth. The truth totally set me free.

There are about 4.6 million children in our country with some kind of disability and more than 50 million people with disabilities. All of these families need to know the truth so that they also can be set free from their guilt. I am committed to spreading the truth to everyone I can.

TWO

Roy and Dale

AND WE KNOW THAT ALL THINGS WORK TOGETHER FOR GOOD TO THOSE WHO LOVE GOD, TO THOSE WHO ARE CALLED ACCORDING TO HIS PURPOSE. —ROMANS 8:28

In 2000 Caroline was invited to fly to Victorville, California, to meet renowned cowgirl and beloved actress and singer Dale Evans at the Roy Rogers and Dale Evans Museum. It was a divine appointment.

Dale had inspired me because we both had daughters who were diagnosed with Down syndrome, and now my husband and I and all five of our children had the opportunity to talk for awhile. Then just before leaving she grabbed my hand and quoted Romans 8:28. It was a defining moment for me, and I have held on to it for years repeating the Scripture over and over.

I knew I loved God, so I was hanging on to the fact—not the hope—that this situation was going to work out for good. Then no less than seven years later—still meditating on that verse—the word *work* popped out at me. For years I had just focused on the words like *love* and *good*—words that we would rather think about anyway. None of us are naturally driven to think about work. But the more I thought about *"it works together for my good,"* the more sense it all made.

It is similar to how we all love a clean house and a warm meal at the end of the day. You and I both know you can love it and be convinced it is "a good thing," but it still takes work. It's the same principle with God. The difficult situation facing you right now can be turned around by God. He can make it work out for good to be fulfilled in your life. The Lord takes a mountain in your life that came to you through the fall of man, and He uses it along with all the other things in your life to make it work together for your good. Some situations may not seem very good right at this moment, but if you trust God, *it will*. Trust the fact that your heavenly Father is working out every detail in your life for your good.

THREE

The Heart

... FOR THE LORD DOES NOT SEE AS MAN SEES: FOR MAN LOOKS AT THE OUTWARD APPEARANCE, BUT THE LORD LOOKS AT THE HEART. —1 SAMUEL 16:7

During the first year of Caroline's life I was given many books that tried to explain and prepare me for the hundreds of things that could and probably would go wrong with my special child. In great detail experts relayed what she would do late or maybe never do at all. Chapter after chapter laid out the medical challenges my child might endure throughout her entire life. In fact, the books outlined every conceivable negative so I might be properly informed. Needless to say, I was quite overwhelmed by all this negativity.

Yet, what all theses books neglected to share are the thousands and thousands of wonderful things that we would experience with this child—the *treasure we would find* as we walked through life with her.

I still remember the day I pushed her in the cart at Wal-Mart, and she put her little lips together saying *mama*. It was a defining moment of pure joy, and it made my day every time it happened. I cannot even begin to count the thousands of incidents of spontaneous laughter that she has provoked or the joy of so many accomplishments that we would have taken for granted.

Caroline has brought a level of compassion to our family that is priceless. The patience, the understanding and the thousands of others things that I would gain from this one little life also were not mentioned in the books. The unselfish love that I've seen Caroline extend to others has allowed me little glimpses of what I believe God is looking for in our hearts. She truly values others and becomes as excited about someone else's accomplishments as she does her own.

Perhaps books you've been given also forget to tell you that your special child will make you feel alive, and how the most mundane things become thrilling when you watch him or her experience them.

I'm reminded of Helen Keller. It was because of a mother's love and a teacher's determination that she did not have to experience life as it was dictated by a diagnosis. She did not let a book tell her about her life; rather she wrote books and surprised the world with her endless possibilities.

Remember, dear special parents, the real treasures in life are those felt with the heart. So in this sense, I feel that my child truly is a gift from God to let me experience life with my heart.

I have found a treasure.

"THE BEST AND MOST BEAUTIFUL THINGS
IN THE WORLD CANNOT BE SEEN OR EVEN TOUCHED.
THEY MUST BE FELT WITH THE HEART."
— HELEN KELLER

FOUR

High Places

THE LORD GOD IS MY STRENGTH; HE WILL MAKE MY FEET
LIKE DEER FEET. — HABAKKUK 3:19

We all know strength is the one thing mothers cry out for often. I learned that lesson very early on. In fact, the Lord gave me this Scripture when I was pregnant with my second child, not even knowing she would be a special child. Our faithful God began to prepare me.

Many times I pictured deer and how they ascend up a mountain with such confidence and even with joy like the enormous challenge was delightful. Yet, I didn't look at my mountain with any confidence or joy.

I had Caroline (our precious and special little angel) in May, but in December of the same year I found out I was pregnant with twins. At that point the mountain seemed bigger, and I just got weaker. The tasks ahead seemed insurmountable. I still would come across this Scripture and speak it out knowing that the Lord was my strength.

Two years later when I had a five-year-old, a three-year-old and two-year-old twins, I became pregnant with our last child. Having five children in just less than six years made my mountain seem bigger than ever, and all of this made me feel that I was weaker than ever. I was weak, frustrated and feeling a big giant of despair. Have you noticed that when you get tired and overwhelmed the devil doesn't let up on you even a little? He comes at you even harder, like that lion seeking whomever he may devour.

Yet, thank God, Jesus never comes late. He threw me a lifeline, and I tied a knot and hung on. What was it? Well, it wasn't a nanny or a million dollars; it was even better. God sent His Word and it (the Word) healed me. He told me the secret to having all the strength you need: Nehemiah 8:10. The Scripture says, "The joy of the Lord is your strength."

God has plenty of joy, and He sends it your way all day long. So just partake in it. Throw perfection out the window and laugh. When your perfect friend drops in around noon—and you're still in your bathrobe and a dog runs through your house that you aren't even sure is yours—just laugh. You will feel better and stronger, and everyone around you will feel better too. It's the only way you'll make it, and pretty soon you'll find that you're even enjoying it.

Soon people will look at you and ask, "How do you do it?"

"With joy!" you will answer, because joy will be the strength that carries you through.

FIVE

Ever Increasing

MAY THE LORD GIVE YOU INCREASE MORE AND MORE, YOU AND YOUR CHILDREN. —PSALM 115:14

Praise the Lord for the more and more because God intends for us to go from glory to glory. It would be wonderful to go from zero to a million overnight, but that rarely happens. Instead, we grow gradually while always increasing. That is a fact when you walk with God. He gives life and life abundantly—He gives more and more. Notice He is not a stingy God. He has all you need, and He will never run out.

Remember, it is the thief who comes to steal from you (John 10:10). God gives His increase gradually, but if you take notice you'll see that you are moving in the right direction and making progress. It's "line upon line."

As a schoolteacher, I know that children start out in kindergarten knowing very little. Yet, day after day they progress and by their graduation, you're moved to tears. Nevertheless, sometimes in the day-to-day of life we forget to look and see if there is growth.

As the parent of any child, it's easy to get overwhelmed in this competitive world. A special child—or any other child—

should never be compared with another child. God made unique individuals, and we need to celebrate that. Truly, we're going from glory to glory.

Every now and then we look back and think about how hard it was for our child to say that first word. Yet, now she talks all the time—especially since she got her cell phone. So don't look around at the world and measure by those standards. Look to Jesus. Look at what He is doing in you and in your child's life—and jump for joy.

Really, I believe that special parents are the happiest parents on Earth. You should have seen me the day my little treasure, Caroline, took her first steps to get the M&Ms off the couch. I've watched footage of man's first steps on the moon, but still it doesn't rival the excitement in my living room the day she first walked.

Know that the Lord is steadily and faithfully increasing you and your children. Praise Him for even the smallest thing. It is just one of His great promises.

SIX

Kindness

"IS THERE NOT STILL SOMEONE OF THE HOUSE OF SAUL, TO WHOM I MAY SHOW THE KINDNESS OF GOD?" AND ZIBA SAID TO THE KING, "THERE IS STILL A SON OF JONATHAN WHO IS LAME IN HIS FEET." —2 SAMUEL 9:3

David had made a covenant with Jonathan, a promise of kindness in return for Jonathan's kindness toward him. And David, being a man of character, intended to do whatever it took to fulfill the covenant. Even though Jonathan was killed, still David looked for someone in that family to whom he could show kindness.

David began asking, Isn't there anyone I could bless on Jonathan's behalf? A servant named Ziba spoke up about a little crippled boy named Mephibosheth who was Jonathan's son and still alive in the town of LoDebar. David immediately gave orders that young Mephibosheth be brought to the palace. But that was only the beginning.

David also restored to the youth all the land of Saul, and then David ordered that the boy would eat at the king's table for the rest of his life. The boy suddenly found himself in the land of plenty. You see, David had a heart after God, and God's heart is to take care of His own with great provision.

Please take note that David did not care that Mephibosheth was crippled. He didn't care at all because, after all, a promise is a promise. David intended to show God's kindness to that family just like any other family.

Like Mephibosheth our children also have a covenant that is theirs. Our children have a promise of blessing from God Himself. God is looking for all those in His family to whom He can show kindness. Your child may have more to overcome than the average child, but that certainly does not mean he or she is left out, cursed or forgotten. He or she is under the same blessings that are promised to you and me.

I've seen God go out of His way to bless my daughter. While I was still pregnant, a woman (I barely knew) felt the Lord wanted her to bless me, and every little bit I would receive a check in the mail or some kind of blessing. Neither the woman nor I knew that Caroline would have special needs, but I know in my heart that the Lord was saying even before she got here that He wanted to show her kindness. And He's never quit blessing yet.

Please know in your heart that God loves your child! Expect Him to go out of His way to bless your son or daughter just like King David went out of his way to find and bless Mephibosheth.

SEVEN

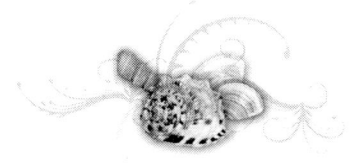

Speak Life

DEATH AND LIFE ARE IN THE POWER OF THE TONGUE, AND THOSE WHO LOVE IT WILL EAT ITS FRUIT. — PROVERBS 18:21

As parents we choose life for our families and ourselves. In fact, in John 10:10 God promises not only life, but also life abundantly. Yet, we must discipline our tongues to eat its fruit.

Even when the circumstances and situations in life call for you to speak negatively about your family, remember we walk by faith and not by sight (1Corinthians 5:7). The Bible says that faith is the substance of things hoped for (Hebrews11:1), so it's important for you to speak what you *hope for*—*not* what you actually see.

In fact, God's Word says we should speak those things that are not as though they are (Romans 4:4). Do you realize that simply amounts to believing what God's Word says about your situation over what your five senses tell you?

For example, sure—you might have received a negative diagnosis about your child from a doctor. Yes, sure, you understand the diagnosis and all its ramifications. But you do not have to agree with its verdict. After all, God has the last word in your life and the life of your child.

Continually speak good things over that wonderfully made child of yours, knowing that life and death are in the power of your tongue. Look for reasons to praise your children, and watch life bloom. You will feel better, and so will they. And by and by, you will see the very things you speak come to pass.

EIGHT

Joy Will Come

... WEEPING MAY ENDURE FOR A NIGHT, BUT JOY COMES IN THE MORNING. — PSALMS 30:5

We all know as children of God that our complete joy will come when Jesus Christ returns in the clouds to call us to our heavenly home. But meanwhile here on Earth, sometimes we cry and sometimes the nights seem very long. Thank goodness joy comes in the morning.

I believe the devil fights us mentally, emotionally and physically—not just spiritually. As any parent can tell us, the devil doesn't let up just because we're tired. In fact, he knows a person is at his or her weakest when he or she is tired, and he attacks all the more. Yet, the Word says that we are not unwise to his schemes.

It seemed like for a while he attacked me harder at night when I was exhausted and needed my rest for the next day. I would spend half the night crying, and then in the morning I was too physically and emotionally tired to do my best. After quite a few years of this, I began to realize his battle plan. So I found all kinds of Scripture to fight him when he came at me at night.

I called him a liar and the father of all lies; I called him the accuser of the brethren, which he truly is. One thing I found works best and yet seems too easy: I simply started ignoring him. At first he kept me up all night torturing me. Then I would stay up fighting him, but in both cases I woke up tired. The truth is, a tired enemy is easily defeated.

So now I recognize him and his tricks, and I speak the Word. Then, I simply turn over and go to sleep. Surprisingly, I wake up rested and ready for the day. And joy comes.

NINE

Fall in Love

GOD IS LOVE. — 1 JOHN 4:8

Love is the oil that makes life work.
When you think about it, anything and everything are more difficult when you dislike doing them. People are difficult to be around unless you love them because love covers a multitude of sins. So really, perfection is not the problem with anyone or anything. It all comes down to a love issue.

That's why at least two commandments are only complete in love: Love God with all your heart, and love your neighbor as yourself. So quit trying to make everyone and everything perfect. Simply let go and fall in love.

Get out those rose-colored glasses the Lord gave you when you were first saved, and you will remember how beautiful the world and the people He put in it really are. Look at everything through the eyes of love.

Faith works by love, which is one reason the devil wants you to get out of your love walk. God is in you, and He is love. So all the love you need *is already* in you! At times you may not feel like it—and you may be tempted not to act like it—but if you're born again, the love of God *is* in you.

In fact, Romans 5:5 says, "...For we know how dearly God loves us, because he has given us the Holy Spirit to *fill our hearts with his love*" (NLT). *Filled* isn't just a little dab, that's a whole lot of love. More than enough to spread around to others!

TEN

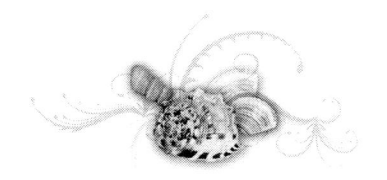

Your Redeemer is Alive

FOR I KNOW THAT MY REDEEMER LIVES.... —JOB 19:25

It's a great revelation to know that your Redeemer lives! According to Hebrews 13:8, Jesus Christ is the same yesterday, today and forever. That means the same Jesus is alive and well. That's good news! Remind yourself that God is still good and still doing business.

The Bible tells of a man named Job who was in the middle of a big mess and could not answer all of the questions in his mind or the minds of his friends. But he did know one important thing. He knew his Redeemer lived. Emotions will come and go, but Jesus never changes.

"Why do the wicked live on, growing old and increasing in power? They see their children established around them, their offspring before their eyes." Job asked in (Job 21:7-8 NIV), as he dealt with his emotions. Deep down his spirit was sure his Redeemer still lived, but a part of Job wasn't so sure the world was fair. Haven't you ever felt that way? If you're the parent of a special child, sometimes you might look at the world and think things don't seem fair. Yet, we must speak out what we know in our spirit—that our Redeemer lives.

Jesus will redeem for you what Satan stole through the curse, and you will receive back what is rightfully ours. Speaking in the middle of all his losses, Job still knew that God would redeem for him what the devil stole. And we also must speak in the same faith—fully convinced that our Redeemer lives.

ELEVEN

Do Not Worry

THEREFORE DO NOT WORRY ABOUT TOMORROW.... —MATTHEW 6:34

As Christians we all know the Ten Commandments and that violating them will bring a consequence from God. For instance, the consequence of adultery can cause division or divorce in a home. The consequence of coveting brings about unthankfulness toward the blessings of God. So we clearly understand that breaking God's law brings negative consequence.

Here in Matthew 6, Jesus has given us one of His new commandments: Do not worry. This is a tough one to get a hold of for many parents who mistake worry as a sign of caring. Jesus doesn't agree.

He said, "Casting all your care upon Him, for He cares for you" (1 Peter 5:7). Parents sometimes feel that the mental work of worry will produce a positive result. But that cannot be true because breaking a commandment can only bring negative results. Only bad things result from disobeying God's Word.

So what should we do instead of trying to cross bridge after bridge and figure everything out? We must enjoy today, and trust God with tomorrow. Many parents would have extra time to devote to their families if they gave up worrying.

In Matthew 6:33, Jesus said seek first the kingdom of God and His righteousness and *all* these things will be added unto you. I think *all* covers everything you could ever worry about. So break the habit of worry that steals your joy, and focus on the kingdom of God, which brings life and life abundantly.

TWELVE

Nothing Is Impossible

... WITH MEN THIS IS IMPOSSIBLE, BUT WITH GOD ALL THINGS ARE POSSIBLE. — MATTHEW 19:26

Jesus spoke these words, and once again, His words amaze us. Jesus did not hold back when He spoke because He knew God. He was there with God at the creation of the universe, and He's here with us now. He knows that our mountains are nothing to God.

The older I get the less impressed I am with people, and the more I am in awe of God. So get your eyes off of people! They are not your answer, and definitely get your eyes off the mountain, looking instead at the completely matchless face of Jesus. As the old song goes "...and the things of earth will grow strangely dim."

Jesus knew God the Father and that is why He knew that all things were possible to Him. In just the same way, the more you know God—His character, nature, power, love and a million other wonderful things about Him—the more you will believe in Him.

In fact, the longer you look at Jesus, the smaller your problem will become. So seek to know God in all His goodness and how awesome He is, and your problem will vanish in His presence.

"Although the world is full of suffering, it is full also of the overcoming of it."
—Helen Keller

"Did I not say to you that if you would believe you would see the glory of God."
—John 11:40

THIRTEEN

A Firm Foundation

WHO COMFORTS US IN ALL OUR TRIBULATION, THAT WE MAY BE ABLE TO COMFORT THOSE WHO ARE IN ANY TROUBLE, WITH THE COMFORT WITH WHICH WE OURSELVES ARE COMFORTED BY GOD. — 2 CORINTHIANS 1:4

This Scripture is the very heart of why I wrote this daily devotional. As a mother of five children and all with special needs (Doesn't everyone have special needs?), I know the places our minds and emotions can go. When circumstances with special children arise and condemnations flood your mind, it's a lonely place to be.

Every time Jesus reached down and picked me up with the unchanging Word of God, it was always exactly the Word I needed. He often "sent His word and healed me" (Psalm 107). He took the curse for me (Galatians 3:13). And He answered the question: "Who sinned, this man or his parents that he was born blind?" (John 9:2). These are only a few of His Words that have literally saved my life.

People can say many things, but when you receive help from the Word of God that is something you can stand on.

It is a firm foundation—not sinking sand.

"How Firm a Foundation" was my favorite song as a little girl. Its lyrics say, "When through fiery trials thy pathway shall lie, My grace all sufficient shall be thy supply." It is God's grace that saves us, keeps us and leads us on. It is in these few devotions, with my whole heart, I look to comfort you in the same way God's Word has lifted and comforted me.

FOURTEEN

Walk by Faith

WE WALK BY FAITH, NOT BY SIGHT. —2 CORINTHIANS 5:7

Is everything you see in a mess? Are the mountains in your life so big that you cannot even see around them? Remember what you see or feel has nothing at all to do with the truth. As Christians, we must walk by faith and not by sight, and we know that faith cometh by hearing and hearing by the word of God (Romans 10:17).

My husband, John, loves to quote Smith Wigglesworth a lot. Rev. Wigglesworth was a renowned minister in the early 1900s who had such astounding results in his services that he was called "the apostle of faith." There are reports that 23 people were actually raised from the dead during his ministry. So, like my husband, I'm interested in anything the man had to say. Rev. Wigglesworth once made this statement, "I am not moved by what I see. I am not moved by what I feel. I am only moved by the Word of God." Those are true and powerful words.

After all, God's Word is the only truth. Do you feel like your healing will never come? The Word says by Jesus' stripes you are *already* healed (Matthew 8:17; Isaiah 53:4-5). Do you feel forsaken by God? Jesus said that He would never leave you or forsake you (Hebrews 13:5). Do you feel like you are under a curse? Galatians 3:13 says, "Cursed is everyone who hangs on a tree, and Jesus redeemed me from the curse of the law. He took the curse for me."

So keep walking, and do not pay attention to what you see. Believe the Word, and speak what you believe. The things that are seen are temporary (they are going to change), but the things that are not seen are eternal (2 Corinthians 4:18).

FIFTEEN

Wait Eagerly

... IF WE HOPE FOR WHAT WE DO NOT SEE, WE EAGERLY WAIT FOR IT WITH PERSEVERANCE. — ROMANS 8:25

Eagerly wait.... Think about those words for a moment. Waiting is usually quite boring and sometimes even aggravating. Yet, when I wait for something I'm excited about, I wait in a completely different way.

When I used to wait for my husband to get home, I would put on lipstick or perfume, make a good meal and usually look out the window 50 to 100 times. Think about when you are waiting for a baby to be born. You paint the room and make baby blankets, and people throw parties because you're waiting in excitement. There's such a difference in waiting and eagerly waiting.

If you're like me, your hope is in the promise of 1 Peter 2:24, which says, "by whose stripes you were healed." You're hoping and eagerly waiting for the manifestation of that promise for your child. So wait eagerly with perseverance, and don't give up. Prepare for it, get excited about it, see it through the eye of faith and know that a great thing is on the way.

"The enthusiasm of a woman's love is even beyond the biographer's"
—*Jane Austen*

"And now abide faith, hope, love these three; but the greatest of these is love."
—*1 Corinthians 13:13*

SIXTEEN

The Fight of Faith

NOW FAITH IS THE SUBSTANCE OF THINGS HOPED FOR, THE EVIDENCE OF THINGS NOT SEEN. —HEBREWS 11:1

Are you hoping for something? Do you have a list of seemingly unanswered prayers? Does the devil continually tell you they will never happen? Then it is time to begin the fight of faith. Many people forget we are in a war, and it is not against flesh and blood.

Often I feel like a boxer just getting beat black and blue by the devil. Remember, he never lets up because you are wounded; he is out to finish you off. He wants you so mad at God or life or friends that you just quit. So don't ever give up! Raise those gloves and with all the faith in you, hit him with the truth.

Faith, which comes from the Word of God, proves the devil a liar every time. I love the Scriptures that say Jesus made a public spectacle of him when He came out of the tomb. The devil knows he is defeated; we just need to remind him. Jesus conquered death, and God put everything under His feet. The devil is defeated, and it is good to laugh at the enemy. Go ahead and laugh because the joy of the Lord is your strength.

You always fight a liar with the truth, and our truth is God's Word. That is my substance; that is my piece of paper that guarantees me what I am promised. It says my children will be saved in Act 16:31, and by His stripes they are healed according to Isaiah 53. There are thousands of promises in my Good Book.

Faith comes by hearing and hearing by the Word of God. Let me encourage you to hear more and more of God's Word so faith can rise in your heart. Everything good that ever happened to me happened by faith. Get your faith (your evidence), and fight for what is rightfully yours!

There is an old song that goes:

> Look, ye saints! The sight is glorious.
> See the Man of sorrows now.
> From the fight returned victorious,
> Every knee to Him shall bow!
>
> — Thomas Kelly

SEVENTEEN

Truth Versus Lies

GOD IS NOT A MAN, THAT HE SHOULD LIE.... — NUMBERS 23:19

This Scripture has been very valuable to me. When I quote a promise from God's Word, immediately the devil comes to say that there's no way on earth that promise could ever be fulfilled for me. It could never happen, he says. Then I pull out my sword, which is the Word of God, and say "God is not a man that He should lie." It works every time!

This is how Jesus fought the devil when He was fasting for 40 days, and the devil began to test and tempt Him. The devil harassed Jesus when He was the weakest, and he'll come to you when you're at your weakest.

Yet, over and over Jesus answered the devil's taunts saying, "It is written." It is written! Finally the devil was convinced that Jesus believed what He said and left Him alone. Jesus then went on to start His ministry that changed the entire human race.

The more you know God, the more you'll understand that God is not a man that He should lie. That is when you'll start speaking the Word with confidence, and that is what really scares the devil. God's Word mixed with faith is what changes everything.

The more you get to know God, the more you'll see His faithfulness and goodness and all the other characteristics that will convince you that God is not a man. Then you will speak the Word with even greater authority.

"...Remember the words of the Lord Jesus, that He said, 'It is more blessed to give than to receive.'"
—*Acts 20:35*

"For where your treasure is, there your heart will be also."
—*Matt 6:21*

EIGHTEEN

God Meant It for Good

BUT AS FOR YOU, YOU MEANT EVIL AGAINST ME; BUT GOD MEANT IT FOR GOOD.... —GENESIS 50:20

The people in my life who have ministered the most to me have always been the ones who faced a mountain and overcame it. The first few years of my daughter's life, I felt pretty sorry for her, and to be honest, I felt quite sorry for myself also.

Some years ago I began studying the life of Joseph and saw the tremendous power of trusting the Father and how I could use it for my good. Through the fall of Adam many things have come upon us that the devil means to use for evil. Yet, if you keep the right attitude and keep your heart right, God only means things for good and will use them for good. Like Joseph, you might find yourself empowered to feed many.

Really, our misfortune is our fortune. It is the refiner's fire that makes us more valuable. There are two kinds of people: victims and victors. Victims continually rehearse all their difficulties and tend to use them for an excuse not to succeed.

Victors look at the mountain and are almost excited to start the climb because they know through Jesus Christ they can do all things.

I'm convinced that the very struggle that we feel is impossible will become our platform to glorify our Savior. To bring glory to God is the reason we live. Every mountain is different, but Jesus deserves glory in millions of different ways, and our lives are one of the ways.

Choose to be a victor like Joseph. Even though he was betrayed by his brothers, imprisoned by his employer and forgotten, he trusted God through it all. Because he kept his heart pure and his eyes on God, his whole family was saved and so was an entire nation. In one day he went from the prison to the palace. Never underestimate how you handle your difficulties. It may be the very thing God uses to raise you up.

NINETEEN

How to Receive Your Inheritance

... IMITATE THOSE WHO THROUGH FAITH AND PATIENCE INHERIT THE PROMISES. — HEBREWS 6:12

Before you can have your inheritance, you have to know what you've been promised. So let's talk about what's included. You have so many benefits.

First of all, if you call on the Lord, you will be saved. Salvation is the door by which you enter into all of the other promises included in your inheritance. You've also been given the promise of healing, and the Bible says that whatever you put your hand to will prosper. If you know the truth, the truth will set you free. And these are only a few of the precious promises that belong to us as believers. Yet, in order to inherit these Bible promises, we must imitate those who have received theirs before us.

Think of Abraham and how he received the promise of a child in his old age. We read that he stood in faith to receive a seemingly impossible promise. In fact, we sometimes forget that it took 25 years before Abraham and Sarah held Isaac—the promise—in their arms.

It's your turn to believe and receive the promise. Imitate Abraham, and use your faith and your patience. Remember Noah and how he received his promise; imitate him. It was 125 years until he saw what God had promised him. There isn't enough paper to tell of Ruth, Esther, Job, Daniel and thousands more that you could imitate.

Miracles don't always happen overnight, *but they will happen if you keep trusting God!* We have God's Word on it. We have the guarantee of our inheritance. It will come. You will receive the miracle you are crying out for. Simply trust Him.

TWENTY

Endurance

FOR YOU HAVE NEED OF ENDURANCE, SO THAT AFTER YOU HAVE DONE THE WILL OF GOD, YOU MAY RECEIVE THE PROMISE. — HEBREWS 10:36

Life is not a sprint; it is a marathon. And all of life is one big endurance race.

Actually, the word *endurance* means to continue and to bear up under difficult circumstances. The word actually reminds me of watching the New York City Marathon; I've always been amazed at the endurance of the runners. Once I saw two women literally crawl across the finish line, but praise God, they made it.

No doubt you've realized that in life, especially in difficult situations, you also need to endure. You need to think past the pain and the hurt, and strive for the finish line. The U.S. Marines say it like this: Pain is weakness leaving your body. The Bible says it like this: "I have fought the good fight, I have finished the race, I have kept the faith" (2 Timothy 4:7). Truth is, if you don't quit, you *will* win and receive your promise.

Years ago, while pregnant with twins John and Anna, my daughter, Caroline, was hospitalized at the age of six months old for an entire week. The word *miserable* does not adequately describe how tired and worn out I felt. Trying to curl up with her in the hospital bed at night and dealing with the constant negative reports were almost too much to bear. It was definitely a time of endurance for me.

Many of those days I felt like giving up, but I made the decision not to cave in and give up. I did endure and just like 2 Timothy 4:7 says, I fought, I finished, and I did not give up the faith. Today Caroline is a very grown-up thirteen-year-old. Have I experienced trials since those early days? Yes. Have I given up? Never!

Endure and receive the promise God has given you.

TWENTY-ONE

Hold Fast

LET US HOLD FAST THE CONFESSION OF OUR HOPE WITHOUT WAVERING, FOR HE WHO PROMISED IS FAITHFUL. — HEBREWS 10:23

Do you hope for something? Whatever it is, confess it and do not let go of it. Hold Fast. Hold on. If you've asked the One who is faithful, Jesus, and it lines up with the Word, then it's on the way. Confess it daily and do not waver.

James 1:6-7 says, "But let him ask in faith, with no doubting, for he who doubts is like a wave of the sea driven and tossed by the wind. For let not that man suppose that he will receive anything from the Lord." Think about that for a minute. It says *ask and do not doubt.*

Don't just speak healing, prosperity or deliverance on a sunny day, but even when your ship is being tossed. Remember who is on board with you. Keep confessing without wavering, even if your mind is arguing with your spirit.

Several years ago, I decided in my spirit that our house should be paid for, and yet, at that time we owed hundreds of thousands of dollars on it. My mind immediately began to disagree with my spirit every time I would speak it. In the natural, or by actual facts or circumstances, it made no sense to me. It seemed utterly impossible for a mortgage to be paid off in such a short period of time, but my spirit had fully agreed with God's Word. And according to God's Word, if I confessed and did not waver in my spirit, God would be faithful.

I will never forget the day we sent the money to the bank and paid off the note on the house. What a glorious day! God *is* faithful, if you just *hold fast!* I'm still holding on for many other things that are on the way for our family.

TWENTY-TWO

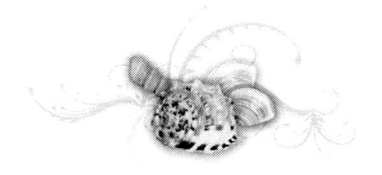

Finding a Treasure

I REJOICE AT YOUR WORD AS ONE WHO FINDS GREAT TREASURE. —PSALMS 119:162

Finding a treasure is one of the most exciting things on Earth. Men and women have been known to travel down to the deepest parts of the ocean to seek hidden treasures, while others stumble across something of great value by complete accident.

No matter—one of the greatest secrets of finding a treasure is recognizing the treasure when you come across it. Hundreds—perhaps thousands—may pass by the same thing, but it's the true seeker who will stop and take note of the treasure's value and receive its reward.

I love antique shows where people bring in their items with great expectations. I'm thinking of one show in particular where individuals excitedly bring their valuable before an expert who will determine if they have a rare treasure. Sometimes these people buy the items at garage sales for pennies while other items were handed down through generations of a family. When the appraiser gives his or her verdict, some people are very disappointed with the findings, while others have their suspicions of treasure confirmed. I especially enjoy the look on a person's face when he or she is told by the expert that the item is an heirloom of significant value.

For me, my special Caroline was like finding a treasure. Actually, the world wasn't sure about her, but deep down inside I was quite sure that she was really something priceless. And God used this little treasure to lead me to the world's greatest treasure—God's Word.

Unfortunately, God's Word is one treasure that is often over looked. It's around us everywhere in bookstores, hotels, libraries and even sitting pretty on coffee tables in many homes. Yet, the world usually passes it by without noticing how precious it really is. I see people in great need seeking help and all the while not realizing the answer to their need is as easy as opening the pages of God's Word. After all, God's Word is what healed me and set me free, and I rejoice over it like someone who has found a great treasure.

Matthew 6:33 says we should seek first the kingdom of God and all these things shall be added unto us. Isn't that good advice? If we'll seek *The Treasure* first, everything else—absolutely everything else—will fall into place throughout our lives. He'll see to it.

TWENTY-THREE

Believing Isn't Pretending

AND NOT BEING WEAK IN FAITH, HE DID NOT CONSIDER HIS OWN BODY.... —ROMANS 4:19

Abraham knew he and Sarah were too old to have children, but he had heard from God. So he considered their ages, but through faith he decided that God was able to do what He said He would do. That is the very essence of faith—knowing what you know about your situation, but choosing to believe God's Word over what you see.

Really, the fact that Abraham and Sarah were too old was obvious to both of them. Yet, Abraham was convinced that God was more reliable than what he could see. He did not pretend the problem did not exist and at times even tried to help God out. Nevertheless, it was through faith that he received the promise.

Consider this: The natural is subject to change if you believe in the supernatural. We are not called to pretend but we are called to believe. God always honors faith. Abraham was accredited righteousness because he believed. What will be accredited to you and me?

You may know very well that your child has been given a diagnosis, but it's important that you choose to consider what God says about the situation as your highest authority. Believing in the power of God to change your circumstances is not pretending. You see, when God comes on the scene everything changes, and it's our faith and trust in Him that causes Him to move. So go ahead and call those things that are not as though they were just like Abraham did (Romans 4:17). It's not pretending—it's believing. It is your faith at work!

TWENTY-FOUR

A New Kind of Fast

IS THIS NOT THE FAST I HAVE CHOSEN: TO LOOSE THE BONDS OF WICKEDNESS, TO UNDO THE HEAVY BURDENS, TO LET THE OPPRESSED GO FREE ... IS IT NOT TO SHARE YOUR BREAD WITH THE HUNGRY ... THEN YOUR LIGHT SHALL BREAK FORTH LIKE THE MORNING, YOUR HEALING SHALL SPRING FORTH SPEEDILY....
— ISAIAH 58:6-8

In the first part of Isaiah 58, it describes fasting like many of us do—painful and self-focused. And God asks, "This is what you think I want?" I want you to go loosen someone bound by sin. Untie heavy loads put on by religion and the world. Tell the oppressed they are set free. Then I will answer you. In others words, you take care of what is on My heart, and I'll take care of what is on yours.

I've learned the more I focus on my problems, the lower I get. Many times my fasting time was completely all about my situation and me. Yet, this Scripture helped me to get my eyes off myself and look to Jesus. And this is what He told me: Look around at the world, and tell them what I did for them. Do what I did, He said. Well, what did He do? He prayed for the sick, fed the poor and visited people in prison. As always, His Word worked.

Jesus may well call us to fast, but here the Bible says that God wants us to get out of our four walls and demonstrate God's goodness. For the past few years, every Friday night our entire family loads a big, green truck with boxes of groceries, and we go into the neighborhoods to teach families God's Word and to pray for people.

The entire family always enjoys ministering together—especially Caroline. She always has a great time filling boxes and planning games for the children. Many times on the day we are going out, I feel so low that I wonder how I can help anyone. But after a few hours of teaching about Jesus and passing out food and hugging lots of little ones, I always come back full of joy.

If you will give what is in your hand—no matter how little it may seem—God will multiply it. So I strongly suggest that this kind of fast may be just what you need.

TWENTY-FIVE

I Will

AND I WILL REBUKE THE DEVOURER FOR YOUR SAKES....
—MALACHI 3:11

The previous verse in Malachi says, "Try Me now and see...." I love that part. Jesus is saying try it, and I will take care of that devourer who is continually trying to steal, kill and destroy from anyone he can. I will rebuke him, God said.

As a third-grade teacher, I find very interesting the effects the school principal has on any room he enters. His very presence stops all foolishness and disobedience. The children know that if he catches whatever they're doing, they will have to stop and suffer the consequences of their actions. His authority in our school is evident.

By the same token, Jesus is instructing us to tithe, and He promises He will bless us and rebuke the devourer for our sakes. The higher the authority, the more people who feel the rebuke. So imagine being rebuked by God. When Jesus died on the cross, He was seated at the right side of God. He put everything, including the devil—especially the devil—under His feet and ours. The demons of hell tremble at His very name because they don't want to be rebuked by Him.

Tithe, and give of your first fruits, and stand on this promise. Then every time that thief comes around to take anything that is yours, He'll be stopped.

TWENTY-SIX

Perfect Love

... WITH HIM ON MY SIDE I'M FEARLESS, AFRAID OF NO ONE AND NOTHING. —PSALM 27:1 THE MESSAGE

It's a known fact that people are drawn to others who are loved and accepted. That euphoric sense of well being draws people to them. Truly, people will not follow a negative person.

Ronald Reagan was one on the most popular presidents of modern times, and one resounding quality he demonstrated in his life and in his speeches was his optimism. He conveyed the sense that nothing was too hard and that as Americans we could succeed. He stood for our country with such a positive stance that Americans were energized and encouraged simply by listening to him.

God knows that we all need that kind of love in us in order to be able to change the world. When we really comprehend how much God loves us, then we'll realize there's nothing to fear. The old saying is true: There is nothing to fear but fear itself. Fear cripples and distorts us, and it tries to prevent us from being the strong leader God expects us to be. He sent His Son to die to redeem every one of us and desires that we live life to the fullest.

Let God's love work in you and through you to cast out fear in every area of your life. Truly, with God you can be fearless—afraid of no one and nothing. You can rise up to be the strong leader God destined you to be.

"The time has come to turn to God and assert our trust in Him for the healing of America. ... Our country is in need of and ready for a spiritual renewal...."

—*Ronald Reagan*

TWENTY-SEVEN

Breakfast of Champions

... TAKE, EAT; THIS IS MY BODY WHICH IS BROKEN FOR YOU. ...
—1 CORINTHIANS 11:24

Recently I heard that a famous athlete ate 10,000 calories for breakfast. That is more than I eat in several days, but the differences between this athlete and me is the amount of calories that are burned. When a body is as active as his, it requires more calories to sustain it and many more to grow stronger.

Years ago when treating a person who had been severely burned, doctors would administer between 2,500 and 3,000 calories a day. That should have been enough to sustain the person. Yet, it wasn't until a former burn victim unexpectedly spoke up that doctors realized differently. The man announced that he had been very hungry throughout the entire healing process, and as a result doctors discovered that people who are healing require many more calories than normal. Because the bodies of these burn victims were repairing tissues and being restored, doctors ultimately realized they needed twice and sometimes three times as many calories as a healthy person.

The same principle applies to your life if you're going through a time where you've been severely hurt or wounded in your spirit. You cannot make it on a small amount of Scripture each day. If your spirit took a blow, then in order to heal quickly—or even just make it—you need more than enough of God's Word. Fortunately, our God is the God of more than enough. One of God's names is *Jehovah Jireh*, meaning He will provide exceedingly, abundantly all you need.

How do we tap into this resource of God promises? Just like your body requires additional calories to heal, your spirit requires big doses of His Word to overcome the storms of life. Our tendency as human beings is to turn inward and hide, but this is the time you should dig into God's wonderful Word and reach out for fellowship with friends and family who can encourage and love you.

Jesus knew His disciples would face incredible challenges after He went to the Cross. He took them to the upper room to share the most important meal in the history of mankind. He told them to take and eat the bread. This was not a meal to fill their stomachs; it was a meal that represents the importance of consuming the Word of God that will make provision for everything you and I need.

Jesus is the Word made flesh, and as we read, study, memorize and quote His wonderful promises each day, we will have more than enough Word on the inside to live in victory over life's circumstances. Remember, greater is He that is in you than He that is in the world!

TWENTY-EIGHT

Come and Worship

AND BEHOLD, A LEPER CAME AND WORSHIPPED HIM....
—MATTHEW 8:2

Around Christmastime all I can sing is that great old song, "O Come, Let Us Adore Him." I just keep thinking...come old, come young, come sick, come healthy and adore Him. *Everyone* come and worship Christ Jesus our King. Come and forget about yourself and just worship.

Wise men and shepherds came to a small stable after Jesus was born to worship Him because He is worthy. Wise men continued to worship Jesus during His earthly life. And wise men and women still worship Him today.

In Matthew 8 we read about a leper who came to worship Him. It's quite a story because lepers were labeled outcasts by society, and it was a pure miracle that the man was bold enough to press past the rejection and rebukes to find Jesus and worship Him. Obviously the leper had it in his heart to worship Jesus. Certainly, it changed him. The man came to Jesus a leper, but left Jesus a completely healed man.

We were all created to worship Jesus, and there is a void in every spirit that's only filled by worshiping Him. It cannot be filled by friends, family, money or even a healing. No. It's only filled by worshipping Him. Don't ever let a label from the world prevent you or anyone in your family from worshipping Jesus.

"You have not lived today successfully unless you've done something for someone who can never repay you."

—*John Bunyan*

TWENTY-NINE

The Next Level

... BUT BRING THEM UP IN THE TRAINING AND ADMONITION OF THE LORD. — EPHESIANS 6:4

As a parent and a teacher of a special child it's important to acknowledge your child's ability level, but still help him or her grow in every area. Isn't that what you expect for every child?

My goal for my special daughter always has been to have expectations that are similar to the expectations I have for my other children. I have empathy and understand when things may be out of her reach, but if I had no expectations at all it would be sympathy. My husband brought Ephesians 4:6 to light for me. It says to bring our children up *in training and admonition. Admonition* is to gently criticize or warn, and by daily *training* she is rising to a new level.

Recently at our school the principal very kindly approached me one day explaining that Caroline was not keeping her shirt tucked in, which is a rule at our school. At first I wanted to respond defensively and say, "Come on! Look, she's doing the best she can." But after walking back to my classroom, I submitted my emotions to the Word of God and chose to humble myself. I quickly decided, *She can do that!* Now she tucks her shirt in just like all the other students, and this admonition and training elevated her to the next level.

Jesus is our standard, and if we allow Him to lead us, we'll all step up to the next level.

"Worship is not about a place, a time or even a song. True worshippers of God worship from the heart with sincerity and truth."

—*Pastor Billy Joe Daugherty*

THIRTY

Prophecy Comes to Pass

FOR UNTO US A CHILD IS BORN, UNTO US A SON IS GIVEN....
—ISAIAH 9:6

... BEHOLD, THE VIRGIN SHALL CONCEIVE AND BEAR A SON....
—ISAIAH 7:14

On Christmas morning all the words of the prophets ring in my ears. Oh, the wonder of it all. Hundreds of years before Christ was born God spoke through men about Jesus. "And out of Egypt I called My son" (Hosea 11:1). Here and above are just a few of the prophecies from the Old Testament. There are many more.

While reading I cannot help but think how millions of people on the Earth and down through history have chosen to believe that Jesus was just another man and not the Son of God. How could that be? After all, these prophecies are recorded in God's Word, and His Word always comes to pass. Hundreds of years passed and some people forgot and some people chose not to believe, but that did not change what was written. There has always been a remnant of believers.

Two people who did not cease to believe were Simon and Anna. They knew God's Word, and they knew by the Holy Spirit that they would see the promised Child. And they did. They chose to believe and not quit.

You also can choose to believe and not quit. What is written in God's Word *will* come to pass. It cannot return void because God Himself said those words, and He is not a man that He should lie (Numbers 23:19). In 1 Kings 8:56 the Bible says, "There has not failed one word of all His good promise…."

Just as sure as you know, along with many other Christians, that Jesus Christ was born of a virgin in a manger, you also need to know He died to set you free. He took stripes for your healing. Even though the promise tarries—*wait for it*—and like Anna you will see the promise come to pass.

THIRTY-ONE

What Kind of Women . . .

THEN JESUS ANSWERED AND SAID TO HER, "O WOMAN, GREAT IS YOUR FAITH! LET IT BE TO YOU AS YOU DESIRE." AND HER DAUGHTER WAS HEALED FROM THAT VERY HOUR. — MATTHEW 15:28

What kind of women follow Jesus? Desperate women. Women who realize that no one else can help them but Jesus.

The woman with the issue of blood wasted years and all the money she had following others. Mary Magdalene had been disappointed by every man she met until her encounter with the King of Kings, Jesus. There isn't enough paper to tell of all the women who received miracles from Jesus by not giving up.

The woman we read about in Matthew 15 also needed a miracle, and so she humbly came to Jesus. Drawing out her faith, Jesus pointed out that bread was only for the children of Israel. Then realizing she was not a Jew, the woman boldly responded to Jesus, saying, "Even little dogs eat the crumbs that fall from their master's table." Desperate people are not easily offended.

Full of compassion and obviously moved by her humility, Jesus said, "Oh woman of great faith." That's quite a compliment from Jesus because He didn't use the phrase *great faith* often. The woman really did have great faith. She may not have had a ministry or a television show teaching about faith, but nevertheless, she was one of the select few throughout Scriptures whom Jesus declared to have great faith.

Great faith has nothing to do with who you are, what family you came from or even what qualifications you have. It's all about knowing who Jesus is. This mother had great faith in Jesus, and her daughter was healed that very hour.

Humble yourself, and exalt God. Faith is not a reward for good behavior—you could never be perfect enough. Faith is simply knowing who Jesus is and what He did. Reach out with the hand of faith to receive what you need!

THIRTY-TWO

All Things

> AS HIS DIVINE POWER HAS GIVEN US ALL THINGS THAT PERTAIN TO LIFE AND GODLINESS THROUGH THE KNOWLEDGE OF HIM WHO CALLED US BY KNOWLEDGE AND VIRTUE. —2 PETER 1:3 (KJV)

Have you ever wondered how you can tap into God's divine power? You do it through the knowledge of Him.

You see, God "knows the things we have need of" both in the natural and supernatural. The Scripture also says by His divine power He gives us all things pertaining to life and godliness. He knows your heart needs to be healed, but at the same time He knows you need a new car. His divine power can accomplish both. God knows how to take care of you inside and out. So how do you tap into this divine power? You do it through the knowledge of Him—through His exceeding great and precious promises.

A few years ago my husband decided to go to Bible school, which I did not really understand. We have five children and a business to run, so this did not make sense to me from a natural standpoint. Yet, the Lord led me to this Scripture in 2 Peter, which says that God will give all things according to our knowledge of Him. John learned so much of the Word that we both became consumed by it.

We grew in our knowledge of Him, and much to our surprise, we began to pay off all of our bills. We paid off our house and all of our bills in less than two years. We became completely debt free. Now tell me that is not divine power. Yet, it all came through our knowledge of Him. Jesus supernaturally gave us the power for life and godliness.

Now it's your turn. Dive into God's Word and learn all you can about our *great God*.

THIRTY-THREE

Wait for the Perfect Timing

THE TIME IS FULFILLED, AND THE KINGDOM OF GOD IS AT HAND. REPENT, AND BELIEVE THE GOSPEL. — MARK 1:15

Have you ever heard that timing is everything? Well, it may not be everything, but it's certainly important to God. He is a God of order, and after all, He did create time. So consider this. If there's a certain time for something, there's a time to wait for that thing.

Jesus had the highest calling of anyone who ever walked on the Earth, and yet, He had to wait thirty years before His ministry began. Waiting is a part of life. Then after waiting all those years, Jesus was driven into the desert and tempted. Waiting is hard enough without the old devil coming up with an entire arsenal of ways to distract and harass Christians. But I'm so thankful that our Jesus came through without a single sin. He knew the kingdom of God was at hand, and He loved us so much that He triumphed over Satan.

We're made in the image of God, and if Jesus recognized God's supernatural timing, then so can we. No one likes to wait. We put in our offering, and we want our harvest the next week. Yet, the Word of God says there is seed time and harvest.

So wait.

When we plant seeds of God's Word in our children, we want to see immediate results. But it usually doesn't work that way, and what we need is to trust that God's Word is working so that it can continue working. We have God's promise that His Word will not return void or empty. We need to wait for it.

God has been so patient with me, waiting sometimes many years for me to change in just one area of life. Amazingly, He never gets upset with us; His long suffering is matchless. We need to match His long suffering with a little of our own.

"So do not throw away this confident trust in the Lord. Remember the great reward it brings you! Patient endurance is what you need now, so that you will continue to do God's will. Then you will receive all that he has promised" (Hebrews 10:35-36, NLT).

THIRTY-FOUR

Set Free!

YOU SHALL KNOW THE TRUTH, AND THE TRUTH SHALL MAKE YOU FREE. —JOHN 8:32

The truth is my whole passion in life. It set me free when nothing else could. And let's face it. We must know the truth in order to live a good life—otherwise, we are living one lie or another.

The first step to real freedom is realizing that Jesus *is* the truth. Scripture says that Jesus is the way, truth and the life. Really, that wraps it all up. It's simple, yet it's also profound. If you don't personally know the truth—Jesus—then lies will keep you from living life abundantly.

Remember, Satan is a liar and the father of all lies. He continually lies to you, and if you don't recognize his voice, you'll be deceived. Yet, if you get in God's Word—and stay in God's Word—you will know who you are and what God did for you. That truth—the whole truth—will make you free in every area of life in every situation you face.

The more you abide in the Word, the more freedom you will have in your life. Our entire battle in life is taking hold of the truth and exposing the lies.

Here are a few scriptures to start you on your journey to freedom.

Lies	Truth
You are rejected.	Ephesians 1:4 says you are chosen.
You are cursed.	Galatians 3:10 says Jesus took your curse.
You are not forgiven.	Romans 10:9 says God has forgiven you.
God cannot heal a sickness.	Psalm 103 says God heals all our diseases.
I caused my child's handicap.	John 9:3 says no man caused this.
Jesus no longer heals today.	Hebrews 13:8 says Jesus is the same forever.

THIRTY-FIVE

Great Peace

ALL YOUR CHILDREN SHALL BE TAUGHT OF THE LORD, AND GREAT SHALL BE THE PEACE OF YOUR CHILDREN. — ISAIAH 54:13

Never underestimate the power of God's Word in any situation, but especially in the heart of your child. Children's hearts are some of the best soil for planting, and I've seen the harvest.

I have five children and from the time they were very little we worked with them to memorize Scripture and plant God's Word in their hearts. I remember them standing against the wall reciting the ABC scriptures. I often added "D" to depart from evil. One of my fondest memories is Caroline doing the hand motions to "Give and it shall be given back to you."

Many times to my surprise *peace* is the word people use to describe our home environment. Imagine that. With five children and a dog that requires a miracle—and the miracle it requires is the Word of God. God's Word is the one thing that can make our lives and our homes peaceful.

Take time with your family to read and memorize the Word of God. When you memorize God's Word, it gets down on the inside of you and your children. Then, when you get squeezed by life's circumstances, what's on the inside will come out. It's definitely the weapon of choice—Jesus Himself used Scripture to combat the devil in the wilderness.

My desire is for my children to be quick to use the Word in everyday life to overcome in times of trial and temptation. God's promise is great peace when your children are taught.

THIRTY-SIX

Follow the Leader

FOLLOW THE WAY OF LOVE.... —1 CORINTHIANS 14:1 (NIV)

As parents and teachers we spend a lot of time teaching our children the best ways in life, and in doing so we use a lot of words. In fact, eighty percent of the words spoken in the classroom are by the teacher. Even with—especially with—our own children, we desperately want them to learn so we talk and talk and talk, some would even say until we are blue in the face.

Yet, I'm not sure our words tell the whole story. I believe the old adage goes a long way toward telling us how children really learn: "Children do as you do, not as you say." And truly, the best way to assess a child is by watching what he or she does.

The little folks watch how we respond in every situation—how we handle a crisis, whether or not we stand up for injustice, and a million other things they're mentally noting. Our children and our students love us so much that they want to be just like us, so we better give thought to the example we're living before them.

Every now and then God gives you a perfect example of this principle. I have one of the most faithful grandmothers helping in my class this year; she is a perfect example. Her little grandson is special in so many ways, and she has brought him to school and stayed there with him from the first bell to the last bell every day since he was in the three-year-old program.

Even at the age of 74, every day she's found helping little people with their lunch trays or opening milk cartons. Whether it's hot or cold outside, every day she makes the playground trip. Her conscientiousness amazes me. As an everyday habit, she gathers lunch boxes and coats the children leave behind and brings them in each day. She's one in a million and a walking, talking testimony of devoted help.

Recently we were very surprised not to see her at school and learned she had to be hospitalized for a few days. We all missed her, and her grandson was very sad. My heart was breaking for him, but the day had to go on, so out to recess we went.

Before long I blew the whistle for the children to come in, but I didn't see her little grandson anywhere. I looked everywhere and still didn't see him. Finally, I saw him. I walked back to the end of the line, and there he stood with lunch boxes hanging off every limb—even his shortened arm.

I understood then. I understood that he had been busy following in his grandmother's footsteps. And I understood that truly our children do what we do—even when we're not there.

THIRTY-SEVEN

Get Over to the Other Side

AND A GREAT WINDSTORM AROSE, AND THE WAVES BEAT INTO THE BOAT, SO THAT IT WAS ALREADY FILLING. — MARK 4:37

Great windstorms seem to come from nowhere and change everything.

At times we've all probably felt like the disciples who climbed in the boat with Jesus and prepared to go to the other side. Like the disciples, we were filled with peace for a safe journey because Jesus was in the boat with us.

But a storm came to the disciples that day—just like it comes to our lives. As the winds began to blow, the disciples became afraid. Fear comes to all of us when we see our lives and loved ones about to drown. In those situations it seems like all the rowing and working in the world cannot help. You know Jesus, but it seems like He isn't responding. That is when we start crying and screaming like the disciples did, "Teacher, do You not care that we're perishing?"

As a teacher and a mother many times I hear that same kind of cry, and we need to respond like Jesus, "Peace, be still!"

Speak peace and help to children when they feel that life is too hard and about to overtake them.

You see, just like Jesus you're the advocate for your children. It's vital that they make it to the other side—for their safety and also because people on the other side are waiting for help. When Jesus and the disciples reached the other side, they found a demon-possessed man who needed a miracle, and he got what he needed because the disciples made it safely.

When your child or you make it to the other side of a difficult situation, there will most likely be someone you can help by saying, "I know the storms of life are real, but I made it and so can you."

THIRTY-EIGHT

Midnight Hour

BUT AT MIDNIGHT PAUL AND SILAS WERE PRAYING AND SINGING HYMNS TO GOD, AND THE PRISONERS WERE LISTENING TO THEM ... AND IMMEDIATELY ALL THE DOORS WERE OPENED AND EVERYONE'S CHAINS WERE LOOSED. —ACTS 16:25-26

Have you ever experienced a *midnight hour?* What did you do? Usually a person's first and most natural reaction is to cry, complain and ask, "Why me?"

But we must check ourselves. After all, will we choose to live according to the natural way of life, being subjected to every circumstance? Or, will we choose to live in the supernatural, rising above circumstances and situations?

Paul and Silas chose to sing and pray during their midnight hour, which caused a mighty earthquake that shook the prison to its very foundation. I want to shake sin and sickness at their very foundation. So instead of crying and complaining, I will sing and pray. How about you?

Do not be tempted to walk in the flesh. Romans 8:13 says if you live according to the flesh you will die, but if you live by the spirit you put to death the deeds of the body and you will live. Like Paul and Silas at midnight when things seem the darkest and we're faced with life and death choices, we must choose. Choose life!

I'd always been a happy person, full of laughter. I always had a song in my heart. Yet, I realized not long after Caroline was born that my song was gone; all I did was cry. One day during my "midnight hour" everything seemed to be so dark and bleak. I was driving, and we were approaching a long bridge. I must be honest I was tempted to give up. The darkness seemed too big.

I knew right then that I had to choose life or death. And I chose life. My three-year-old and I decided to sing every song we could think of about sunshine. By the time we got to the other side of the bridge, I realized my song was back and I could laugh again. Singing set me free! Caroline is thirteen now and one of her favorite things to do is sing. Sing in your midnight hour like Paul and Silas, and watch God throw open the doors.

THIRTY-NINE

Who's Listening?

... AND THE PRISONERS WERE LISTENING TO THEM. —ACTS 16:25

The other prisoners were listening to Paul and Silas sing praises in jail during their midnight hour. Paul and Silas could have been complaining and griping and fighting thoughts of *Why are we here! We don't deserve this!* Instead, they were singing right out loud to the Lord in a dirty and dark prison. Their prayers and adoration to God must have seemed out of place, and yet, amazing to all the other prisoners.

In my midnight hour, I would much rather hear someone praying and praising God then complaining. Many of the parents you will meet in special education classrooms and hospital wards are imprisoned with fear and utter hopelessness, and if you're the parent of a special child you also may feel all of those same emotions. Yet, that's also when you must *choose* to sing!

Like Paul and Silas, sing of God's goodness and pray bold prayers *because* people are listening. Do not join in on the negative conversation. Instead, lift up your head, and praise God in your midnight hour. I love the fact that

Jesus opened all the jailhouse doors that night and *all* were loosened. He shook the whole place and set the prisoners free.

Jesus loves it when we are able to praise Him in the most difficult times. We must also remember, the world is watching and listening to how we respond to tough times. So lift your voice and sing! Let Jesus set you free—and set free all those who are listening and watching.

FORTY

Dig Deep

HE IS LIKE A MAN BUILDING A HOUSE, WHO DUG DEEP AND LAID THE FOUNDATION ON THE ROCK.... —LUKE 6:48

I'm sure many of you sang a little song in Sunday school based on this parable of the wise man who built his house upon the rock. He was pretty wise because he dug deep until he hit rock to lay the foundation for his home. The not-so-wise man began building his house on the sand, and we know what happened to it.

It rained on both homes, but it was not an average spring shower. No, it was a real downpour that flooded the land around both houses. The house on the rock could not be shaken, but Jesus said the other house fell immediately and the ruin of that house was great.

Consider this. Both families built homes, but the most important factor was *how* they built them. The wise man took time to dig deep, and not only heard what Jesus said but did what Jesus said. In other words, both men heard the Word, but only the wise man obeyed and put the Word into action in his life. Anyone can hear and anyone can build. But verse 49 says that he who heard and *did nothing is like a foolish man.*

Let's determine to be doers of the Word so our foundation

will be firm and sure. How do we dig deep? We must obey the Word—forgive, give, walk in faith, go and make disciples. Jesus is our example, and for sure He was a doer of the Word.

The thing is, rain will come to all. You may look at someone who does not have a special child and assume his or her life is bliss, but it rains on everyone. The rain is not the issue at all. Remember, one house stood firm despite the rain. So dig deep until you hit rock. Then by being a doer—not just a hearer only—you'll build on a firm foundation.

FORTY-ONE

A Prophet

... A PROPHET IS NOT WITHOUT HONOR EXCEPT IN HIS OWN COUNTRY AND IN HIS OWN HOUSE. — MATTHEW 13:57

In a Jewish household the father is considered the priest of the home, and he is the primary one who teaches the children their Jewish heritage. In fact, most cultures give great honor and respect to the position of the father.

Unfortunately, I've seen a frightening trend in America lately, where the wife and children treat the father, the head of the home, with little or no respect. If you watch very much television, you'll see the father painted as the ignorant one. I think we are making a big mistake if we agree with the world on this view. God placed the father in the home to guide, help and protect families, and it would be the devil's delight to rob us of this.

I remember a night when our sons had a friend over, and they were being wilder than usual. My husband hollered up the stairs, "Calm down, guys, before someone gets hurt!" Well, in a matter of minutes we heard an awful scream and ran upstairs to find our son, John, on the floor covered in blood. Five stitches and four hours later we were back at home amazed at the "coincidence" that Dad had given a stern warning minutes before.

Actually, we all know that it wasn't a coincidence at all. My husband, John, was doing what God gifted him to do—he was leading his family. And we would have saved time and pain if we would have simply listened and heeded his advice. There really isn't enough paper to write about all the times he was exactly right.

Many times as a girl I knew my dad was right and when I listened I got to eat the fruit of obedience, but several times—determined to get my way—I decided not to listen and regretted it.

Give the prophet of your home the honor that is due him. If you tear down your husband in front of your children they will only see a small dad, but if you build him up they also will honor him.

FORTY-TWO

Family Now

... TO REDEEM THOSE WHO WERE UNDER THE LAW, THAT WE MIGHT RECEIVE THE ADOPTIONS AS SONS. —GALATIANS 4:5

A few years ago I was privileged to go with my brother when he adopted his second child from Guatemala. It was just as exciting as giving birth!

When we first arrived at the orphanage it was overwhelming to see room after room of babies. When I was trying to have a baby I used to say, "There's nothing sadder than a woman who wanted a baby." But after seeing all these babies in need of mothers, I decided it's even sadder to see babies who want mothers.

My brother and sister-in-law have the biggest hearts and knew that the Lord wanted them to have some of their children this way. Once while at my house, my sister-in-law told me that when she was pregnant one of her Guatemalan-born children asked if he had also been in her tummy. And she replied so beautifully, "That she was carrying this baby in her tummy, but she carried him in her heart."

This wonderful demonstration of love made it clear to me what God did to let us become His children. Just like my heart was breaking to see all the Guatemalan babies in need, God looked at the world and knew He had to help. He sent Jesus to rescue us. Jesus left the comfort of His home and redeemed us from the curse that we were born under. God took us as His own, and now He is our Father. We now have all we need because He loved us enough to adopt us.

Every time I see my brother's family, I think how one act of compassion changed these children's lives forever. And I think of how one act of God changed my life forever. I'm so thankful He carried me in His heart.

FORTY-THREE

Hard Pressed

WE ARE HARD-PRESSED ON EVERY SIDE, YET NOT CRUSHED;
WE ARE PERPLEXED, BUT NOT IN DESPAIR. —2 CORINTHIANS 4:8

Do you feel pressed on every side? We've all had those kinds of days—or years—but by some miracle we've made it through to tell about it.

The trouble is, many times we have a whole lot more than a single bad day. Sometimes it's a bad season that seems to beat us down, and it goes on so long we begin wondering if it's just the way life will be for us. Of course, that also leaves us feeling perplexed.

The definition for *perplexed* is a *wondering, confused or entangled*. Sound familiar? That's exactly what the devil has planned for you. He presses on you from every side until he entangles you into believing there's no way out. Actually, there isn't any way out—except Jesus, who's the way, the truth and the life. Jesus is your way out of trouble and your way into life more abundantly every time. Knowing Jesus will keep you from falling into despair.

I met a wonderful little family in the mall one day. They were happier than your average young couple. As we began talking, I found out they had a six-month-old baby who had

Down syndrome. Yet, they tackled every mountain with a smile and always had plenty of love for everyone.

I'm sure it made the devil mad that he didn't slap the joy off them the first time, so he hit them hard again when they found out there were complications with their second child. I saw some despair creep in followed by many tears and questions, but praise God they were not crushed. After many months of testing by the doctors their new little boy was given a clean bill of health. They now have three little boys and are still one of the happiest families I know. What a joy to be around. And what glory they bring to God because they were perplexed but not to despair.

FORTY-FOUR

Take a Walk

FOR WE WALK BY FAITH, NOT BY SIGHT. —2 CORINTHIANS 5:7

I have a full house. My husband works from a home office, and we have five children and a dog. Actually, sometimes we have eight or nine kids depending on where the neighbor children are. So, needless to say, there are times I just want to get out of the house and walk. Really, it's better than staying and saying something I shouldn't. Even when temperatures are freezing, many times I opt to get out and see how big the world is.

If you're in the middle of a mess and life seems to be more than you bargained for, take a walk. In fact, by faith walk right on out into the unseen. Walk out of your troubles, and step into what God has for you. Don't even pay attention to what you see because 2 Corinthians 4:18 says that the things that are seen are temporary.

Would you give someone directions to a house by telling him or her, "There's usually a horse in this pasture so when you see him, turn right?" No! We would never direct someone by things that change from hour to hour. Well, neither does God. And the only things that never change—the only things in this life that are sure and steadfast—are God and His Word. That is why God tells us to walk by faith because it's the only sure way. The Bible says, "Now the just shall live and walk by faith" (Hebrews 10:38).

In 2 Corinthians 4:18, we read that the things that are eternal do not change, but everything else can and will change as we use our faith. So let me encourage you. When everything around you looks like a mess, take a faith walk. Step from one promise to another until you're standing in victory!

FORTY-FIVE

Disbelief

BUT BEHOLD, YOU WILL BE MUTE AND NOT ABLE TO SPEAK UNTIL THE DAY THESE THINGS TAKE PLACE, BECAUSE YOU DID NOT BELIEVE MY WORDS WHICH WILL BE FULFILLED IN THEIR OWN TIME. —LUKE 1:20

One morning while reading this passage about the miracle of John the Baptist's birth, something stood out to me. The Lord sent an angel to tell Zacharias that his prayers for a child to be born had been answered and even greater things would take place with the coming child.

Yet, even though Zacharias and his wife had prayed for a child for years, when the answer came he doubted. And that won't work. God's Word says without faith it is impossible to please Him (Hebrews 11:6). Why is it that we humans cry out for answers and find them in God's Word, but then still doubt? The Word says our children will be saved, healed and rule in this life with authority, and we desire all these things for our children. However, we struggle like Zacharias with doubt.

The angel had a solution to Zacharias' problem and shut his mouth for him. Actually, a lot of us would probably be much better off if our mouths were supernaturally sealed up for awhile until God's promises manifest. If we cannot say yes and amen to God's promises, surely it would be better to be mute.

The truth is, God has already provided every answer we need, and the solution in every situation is for us to believe in our hearts and say with our mouths exactly what God's Word says about our situation. Mark 11:23 says, "For assuredly, I say to you, whoever says to this mountain, 'Be removed and be cast into the sea,' and does not doubt in his heart, but believes that those things he says will be done, he will have whatever he says" (NKJV). So let's be sure to shut our mouths to any unbelief so our faith can set about creating our answers and solutions.

FORTY-SIX

Strong in Spirit

SO THE CHILD GREW AND BECAME STRONG IN SPIRIT....
—LUKE 1:80

John the Baptist was a miracle child born in impossible circumstances to an elderly couple. At last the promised child was born to Zacharias and Elizabeth, and I'm sure their minds soared to the endless possibilities for their son. I know as a parent I even made sure I gave my children names that would be appropriate if they someday were to become president of the United States. I would say their names over and over to see if they sounded presidential.

Most parents have high hopes and expectations for their children. So I'm sure Elizabeth thought, *Hmmm, if I ever have a son, he'll be named after his father.* And yet, the Lord had a different plan and a name for this child. His name would be John, and he would grow up to be used by God and be strong in spirit.

In our generation, we have many considerations for our children. We wonder what career path they will choose and if they're gifted, and toward that end, it's important to us whether or not they're being challenged at school. If they seem physically strong, we may even spend many days and nights in gymnasiums or football fields. Of course, mental and physical development are good—even important—but we must not forget that our children have spirits that also need development. In fact, it's even more important to develop the child's spirit so he or she can grow strong in spirit as John did.

Every child needs to receive salvation, but that's not the end. Actually, it's only the beginning. All of us (even children) have a soul (mind and emotions), live in a body, but we are a spirit. Yet, children are often encouraged to develop their souls and bodies, but the spirit is forgotten.

After being a Christian for many years and feeding my spirit daily, I'm firmly convinced of the benefits of having a strong spirit. I'm also convinced that children grow so fast that parents need to make a conscious effort to train their children to become strong in spirit. *How?* you might wonder. They're spirits grow and develop as they read or memorize Scriptures, hear the Word taught at church, listen to praise and worship music and pray in the spirit. All my children, including Caroline, do all of these things, and the evidence is everywhere. I give all the glory to God, who wants all our children to grow physically and spiritually. He wants everyone one of us to grow strong in spirit.

FORTY-SEVEN

State Your Case

PUT ME IN REMEMBRANCE; LET US CONTEND TOGETHER; STATE YOUR CASE, THAT YOU MAY BE ACQUITTED. —ISAIAH 43:26

When people go before a judge, they're usually under attack or accused of something. The judge will rule or offer up a final judgment on the case after he or she hears all the facts. Yet, in order for defendants to combat their accusers, they must be prepared to defend their rights. Defendants need to have a clear understanding of who their accuser is and what his or her intentions are. Defendants also need to know what their rights are and what belongs to them.

Only then—after having done all the homework—is the defendant ready to state his or her case to the judge. Many cases have been won simply because a clever lawyer brings up a law from the past and proves present-day rights still prevail. Did you realize we're in a court too?

Jesus is the One who will judge the Earth, and He is the One who set the new covenant or laws into motion by taking our place on the Cross. Revelation 12:10 tell us that Satan is the accuser of the brethren, and I think we all will agree that he does plenty of accusing. John 10:10 says that the thief or the devil comes to steal, kill and destroy. So we know who our enemy is, and his intentions are pretty clear.

Yet, God promises you and me forgiveness and healing, and God states in His Word what rightfully belongs to you as a child of God. So when the devil comes along to harass and accuse you, simply go before the Lord and state your case. Remind God of His promises to you daily or even hourly, and watch Him say, "Yes and amen to His Word!"

Knowledge empowers you. So find Scriptures that cover your case and go boldly before the throne. Identify the thief and have him arrested. Take the authority Jesus died to give you, state your case, and you'll be acquitted.

FORTY-EIGHT

Let It Go

BUT IF YOU DO NOT FORGIVE, NEITHER WILL YOUR FATHER IN HEAVEN FORGIVE YOUR TRESPASSES. — MARK 11:26

There is great freedom in forgiveness. In fact, Jesus says in this verse that your eternal freedom depends on it. Jesus died so we would have life here on Earth and eternal life in heaven, but if we choose to hold on to an offence and not forgive, then He will not forgive us. That is very sobering news. I make a point to remind myself every time those wonderful temptations to be offended occur.

My husband is famous in our house for saying, "Tie a bow, and let it go!" There's a real truth there because as long as you hold on to an offense, you're still tied to the awful thing the devil threw at you.

It reminds me of watching a rodeo when a cowboy lassoes a calf. He struggles with it a while, and then he ties it off and lets go of the rope. If the cowboy kept wrestling with the cow, one or both would get totally worn out. Really, that's the devil's motive—he sets people up to steal their time and strength.

Yet, as soon as you let it go, you are free! Even if someone was wrong, free them and get it over with. Isn't that what God did for you? Psalm 103 says He didn't treat us like our sins deserved. So next time an offence comes—and it will come—be prepared. Rope it, tie it up, and let it go. Then ride off into the sunset to enjoy the next great adventure God has for you.

FORTY-NINE

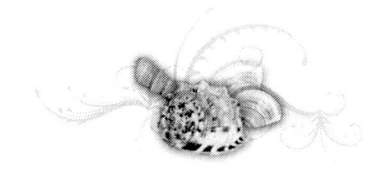

Pass the Test

> THAT THE GENUINENESS OF YOUR FAITH, BEING MUCH MORE PRECIOUS THAN GOLD THAT PERISHES, THOUGH IT IS TESTED BY FIRE, MAY BE FOUND TO PRAISE, HONOR, AND GLORY AT THE REVELATION OF JESUS CHRIST. —1 PETER 1:7

I had the privilege of home schooling my children at different times during their elementary school years, and it was always a joy. We made memories that will last a lifetime. It was a known fact that Friday was testing day, and I generally knew who had prepared and who was trusting. As their mother and teacher, I'd encourage them to study more or prepare, but many times they felt they knew best. Then Friday would roll around and someone would make a fifty percent, and then the tears would fall like rain.

Aren't we all like that in some way? We hear a sermon in church, and we're sure we got it. We don't study or meditate on it, but we feel pretty ready for any test that comes along. Then one of those wonderful life tests does come along and you fail miserably. And the tears fall like rain.

Actually, most of us don't really know what we've received until a test does come along. Life tests our faith in loved ones and even our faith in God. The school of life seems long and hard sometimes, but if we trust God we'll come forth as gold.

Genuine faith is what will give glory and honor to Jesus when He returns, so how privileged we are to be able to offer Him genuine praise tested by fire? When Jesus was put to the test on how much He loved us, He surely came forth like gold. Now it's our turn to pass the test.

FIFTY

Surpassing Peace

AND THE PEACE OF GOD, WHICH SURPASSES ALL UNDERSTANDING, WILL GUARD YOUR HEARTS AND MINDS THROUGH CHRIST JESUS. — PHILIPPIANS 4:7

This promise of peace is preceded by a command to be anxious for nothing, but in everything through prayer with thanksgiving let your request be made known to God. We know from studying the Bible that commands have promises that follow them.

For instance, Abraham obeyed and left his homeland and was blessed beyond his wildest imagination. Another example is to honor your father and mother, which is the first commandment with a promise of long life for those who obey.

Too often, however, we forget that being anxious and worrying is not at all obeying God's commands. What did our text say? *Be anxious for nothing.* In other words, God says not to worry about anything, but to pray about everything. If you cast your care on Jesus, then His supernatural peace will guard your heart and mind. Perhaps you won't be able to understand how you can have peace when you make your request known to Him, but it will come!

A few years ago Caroline was scheduled for a pretty major surgery, and I was engulfed with fear that something would go wrong during the procedure. I went to bed crying out of concern that she would die or lose her eyesight. A spirit of fear was attacking my heart and mind. Unable to stand the fear any longer, I made the decision to fast and pray. I let all my requests be made known to Him. The day of the surgery I had peace that was beyond my understanding.

The truth is that God is able to handle our problems a lot better than we can. So, give Him all your worries, and He will give you all His peace. Once again, what a great trade for us!

FIFTY-ONE

Follow Him

SO WHEN THEY BROUGHT THEIR BOATS TO LAND, THEY FORSOOK ALL AND FOLLOWED HIM. —LUKE 5:11

Being a parent, a spouse, an employee, a friend and a dozen other things are all time consuming. They're all valuable, but they all require time. And for those of us who have a special child, we have yet another calling. Our heart's desire is to function in each role—and wear each hat—with all the best of our ability, but usually our ability doesn't go very far.

So what does God really want from us? He wants us to follow Him! That's it in a nutshell—He wants us to forsake all and follow Him.

Yes, you still need to do the dishes, wash clothes and get up and go to work. You don't quit living! But you must also gather up all your cares and concerns and meet with your heavenly Father heart to heart. Forsake all of your plans, dreams and prayers and simply *seek Him*.

When you abandon all of your hopes and desires as the disciples did, then you will really walk with Jesus. Nothing compares to that. Think of all the disciples saw firsthand because they made the choice to follow Jesus. The disciples' small fishing businesses and their friend and family ties could in no way compare with the taste of heaven they experienced on Earth by following Jesus so closely. You also can experience firsthand the love and the miracles that come with walking closely with our Savior. Matthew 6:33 says, "Seek first the kingdom of God and all these things will be added unto you." How true!

FIFTY-TWO

Power

YOU SHALL RECEIVE POWER WHEN THE HOLY GHOST HAS COME UPON YOU.... —ACTS 1:8

We experienced a catastrophic ice storm here in Oklahoma in 2007. More than 600,000 homes lost power in our state, and the president declared Oklahoma a natural disaster area. Everywhere you looked there were trees down, but the worst part was families were really suffering without power for more than a week. During this time everyone who had a fireplace felt blessed. We were all limited in what we could do and where we could go; the only safe, warm place was in front of the fire.

We will never forget this incident. After a few days our power was restored, and our entire neighborhood was thrilled. The house became warm and lit up again, and we were finally able to move about. We felt like we had our freedom back.

As I was driving to the store, Jesus reminded me of the Scripture about receiving power from the Holy Spirit. During the storm we were limited to huddling around small fires that gave off very little light and only some warmth. But when the power was fully restored, we were warm and moved about freely.

Think about it this way. The Scripture says when you receive power, you can go to the ends of the Earth. Just like my town was cold, dark and in danger without power, the world is in great danger unless we take the power that's in us to them. Whether we head around the world or next door, let's take the power and *go!*

FIFTY-THREE

Diagnosed

AND WHAT IS THE EXCEEDING GREATNESS OF HIS POWER TOWARD US WHO BELIEVE, ACCORDING TO THE WORKING OF HIS MIGHTY POWER WHICH HE WORKED IN CHRIST WHEN HE RAISED HIM FROM THE DEAD AND SEATED HIM AT HIS RIGHT HAND IN THE HEAVENLY PLACES, FAR ABOVE ALL PRINCIPALITY AND POWER AND MIGHT AND DOMINION, AND EVERY NAME THAT IS NAMED, NOT ONLY IN THIS AGE BUT ALSO IN THAT WHICH IS TO COME.
— EPHESIANS 1:19-21

Like me, you'll probably never forget the moment a doctor stood before you and named the disease that would label your child different or special.

I had been in labor all morning, and finally at 2:22 p.m. my Caroline decided to come with a bang. It all happened so fast the doctor barely made it for the delivery. I was so glad to see my chubby baby girl I had waited so long to hold. Too much in pain and too exhausted to notice anything at all, I rested in the fact that the hard part was over.

Yet, later that day I saw doctors and nurses scurrying around and acting a little weird, but again, I was so tired that I quickly dismissed it all. Then in the middle of the night, when many of us are the most tired and confused, a nurse decided to fill me in on everything the doctors and family were thinking. I remember being so tired—but so shocked by this horrible picture she painted of my child—that I'll never forget a word she said.

I thought later, *So doctors ran some tests and named her.* Funny thing, I named her *Caroline*; everyone else labeled her a Down's baby. Wow, that irritated me! She was a little girl not a little syndrome. Suddenly I was facing a pretty big mountain to move, but I knew together with Jesus all things are possible (Matthew 19:26). But first and foremost, I wanted people to quit labeling her as *a problem.*

One day I read a portion of Scripture that said Christ is above "every name that is named" (Ephesians 1:21). Suddenly I realized why it irritated me so badly when people referred to her as a Down's baby. I realized that the same power that raised Jesus from the dead was working in Caroline and me, and no name would exalt its name above His name.

Never stand in fear of the names ADD, autism, handicap, Down syndrome—or any of a hundred other names given by society. Jesus conquered death and is seated far above all these names. Call your child healed and whole and know all these other names are under His feet—and therefore, under your feet as well.

FIFTY-FOUR

Touch Him

... AND [THE WOMAN] HAD SUFFERED MANY THINGS FROM MANY PHYSICIANS. SHE HAD SPENT ALL THAT SHE HAD AND WAS NO BETTER, BUT RATHER GREW WORSE. WHEN SHE HEARD ABOUT JESUS, SHE CAME BEHIND HIM IN THE CROWD AND TOUCHED HIS GARMENT. — MARK 5:26-27

People in the Bible who sought Jesus have always been of special interest to me. Most of them were poor, hungry or sick, so never feel condemned for seeking Jesus because of what you're going through. My heart really goes out to the woman in Mark who had tried everything and only grew worse. She had spent all the money she had, but was no better, the Word says.

I can imagine how she felt. I believe my husband and I have felt like she felt. In fact, from the time Caroline was a baby, we've frequently had people try to sell us some miracle drug in a bottle that would cure everything. I even tried a few and never really saw any change. Like the woman in the Bible, you can spend all your time and money and still not get any better.

Yet, also like this woman, you can hear about a healer and press in to touch Him. One thing is clear: Jesus is *the answer*. There will always be a group saying they have the cure or the answer, but trust me, don't spend all your time, money or energy chasing empty promises. Press in to touch the Healer. As you reach out and touch Him, you'll find everything you need is in Him.

"Healing rain is a real touch from God. It could be physical healing or emotional...."
—*Michael W. Smith*

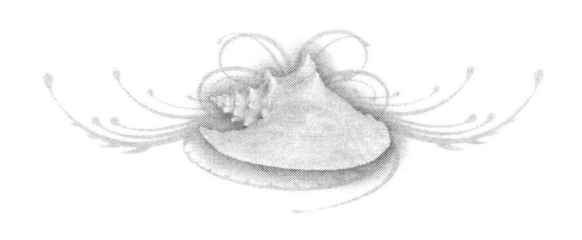

"Success is to be measured not so much by the position that one has reached in life as by the obstacles which he has overcome."
—*Booker T. Washington*

FIFTY-FIVE

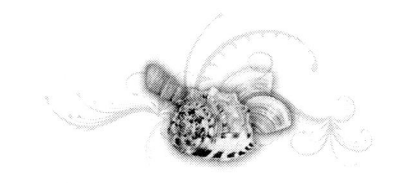

A Strong Consolation

... IT IS IMPOSSIBLE FOR GOD TO LIE, WE MIGHT HAVE STRONG CONSOLATION, WHO HAVE FLED FOR REFUGE TO LAY HOLD OF THE HOPE SET BEFORE US. — HEBREWS 6:18

Have you fled to Jesus to find refuge from the world and its destruction? By faith have you grabbed hold of the hope that God's Word gives us? Then take comfort or console yourself because it's *impossible for God to lie*. All that you hold to—all that you have read in the Scriptures and all the promises you've memorized—will come to pass.

The fact that God cannot lie is a strong consolation. Remember Jesus called the devil the father of all lies, so the war we are in all comes down to this: believing truth or believing lies.

You see, everything in God's Word is true. It is truth that your sins are forgiven; God doesn't even remember them any more. In 1 Peter 2:24 it says by His stripes you were healed. Psalm 1 says whatever you put your hand to will prosper. These are the truths that you can console yourself with, and He is God and cannot lie.

The devil has tricked people into believing they love to sin. He's convinced people that they must take what's dealt to them because God can hardly wait to punish them. Lies. Lies. More lies. All of these are lies. Jesus died to give everyone life and life more abundantly. Take hold of the truth and know that God cannot lie!

Fifty-Six

A Perfect Way

It is God who arms me with strength, and makes my way perfect. — Psalm 18:32

The Lord gave me this Scripture right before I had major surgery a few years ago. I was confident that the Lord said go ahead with the surgery, but still, being under general anesthesia for so long wasn't something anyone would look forward to experiencing. Then again, being a mother of five children, I also wasn't looking forward to the long recovery time. Nevertheless, the Lord showed me this Scripture, and I knew He would see me through.

The day after Mother's Day I went into the hospital with a few tears and went through with the surgery. Like always, our faithful God showed up and armed me with strength and made my way perfect. I was the first woman in Tulsa who was given a new pain treatment after surgery, and it helped me recover without so much pain. Even the doctors were amazed. I knew it was God. If you trust Him, He will work out things perfectly for you.

A few years later, Caroline needed eye surgery, and I really struggled with fear. To be honest, I was tortured with fear day and night so I decided to fast a day before her surgery. Then

God reminded me of this Scripture once again, and as I began speaking it over the situation, fear took flight. All through her surgery I sat in the waiting room with perfect peace. That in itself was a miracle because the week before I had cried myself to sleep every night. But when Dr. Ben (as Caroline calls him) came through the surgery door into the waiting room, He kept saying, "It all went perfect!"

I'm so thankful that the Word of God does not return void. You see, removing cataracts from a child's eyes is much more difficult than removing them from an adult's eyes. But with God, all things are possible! Stand on a specific Scripture and do not waver, and watch God remove every obstacle.

FIFTY-SEVEN

Get Filled Up

... IN YOUR PRESENCE IS FULLNESS OF JOY.... —PSALM 16:11

This generation is seeking to be filled like none before it. People are overeating, overshopping, overtalking and overworking in search of being filled. Too often, they are looking for love in all the wrong places.

If you really want to be full, then get in the presence of the Lord and fill up. Don't tell Him everything He already knows, just drink up His presence. He knows you are tired, He knows your heart is aching, and He also knows that if your joy goes so does your strength. Life tends to steal your joy, and worse yet, sometimes we're tempted to fill up with things that actually end up leaving us emptier.

I love to shop and sometimes it's necessary, but I've also been caught at the mall trying to buy something that might help me regain my joy. But the only thing that mall trip really accomplished was taking my money and time. I've also gotten on the phone and told all my problems to a friend and hung up not feeling any better.

Here's where I've found the real answer. I get up a little early and get in the presence of the Lord and soak Him up! As you wait on the Lord, there's not only a fullness of joy, but also He renews your strength so you can run and not get weary. Don't just run in and run out either, but remain in His presence long enough to get *full* of joy. Then, when you come out full of joy, you'll be able to live a full life the way God has planned for you.

FIFTY-EIGHT

A Virtuous Mother

> SHE OPENS HER MOUTH WITH WISDOM, AND ON HER TONGUE IS THE LAW OF KINDNESS. SHE WATCHES OVER THE WAYS OF HER HOUSEHOLD AND DOES NOT EAT THE BREAD OF IDLENESS.
> — PROVERBS 31:26-27

I hope I never forget the day the tornado alarm went off. I was a little girl of about eight, and we were at school when we heard the dreaded tornado siren. Living in Oklahoma, often times described as Tornado Alley, this was no small event. Even as a child, I recognized from the way everyone was acting that this was not simply another drill.

Teachers were scurrying about and shouting as they quickly ushered us out into the halls and instructed us to put our heads down. We were told to cover and protect our heads with our arms.

Quite simply, I was terrified.

Still to this day, I can vividly remember the cold, hard floor. Even the smell of the hallways marked my memory. But, oh my, most importantly of all, I remember looking up and seeing my mother come quickly around the end of the hall. I've never seen a sight that meant more. I can still see her long dark hair bouncing as she walked quickly carrying one of my brothers in her arms. She had heard the siren blaring, and of course, my mother immediately headed to the school to get her children.

I cannot begin to describe the overwhelming sense of relief I felt. Yet, truly, my mother always showed up when I needed her—then and now.

In these devotions I've shared a lot about the importance of forgiving and forgetting, but there's also a time for rescue—even relief. You see, mothers were created by God for just this job.

My special Caroline has always taken speech even when she was quite small. She would go in and sit in her little chair and give the teacher her best for about fifteen or twenty minutes. But then, nicely and politely, she would stand up and push in her chair and say "I got to go now." I would laugh so hard, but I also knew she had enough for that day.

Actually, fifteen or twenty minutes may not sound like a long time, and yet, I believe all of us in life reach a point when we've "got to go now." We've become tired and overly stimulated, and it seems as though our minds, our emotions and our bodies just cannot tackle another detail. We all know that point when we've just plain had enough. And on that day, little Caroline had had enough. Really—only you know when your child has reached that limit, and it's wise never to override those feelings.

God placed in us—as mothers and fathers—the strong need to protect and preserve our children, and we need to heed our heart's direction. Special education teachers are taught to be advocates for these precious little children, but there's absolutely no better advocate than the child's parents.

Remember, your special child cannot stand up for himself or herself. That's your job! You must show up and speak up on your child's behalf whenever needed. Thank God for the boldness to do it. He'll give it to you because God has placed in your hands His very heart.

FIFTY-NINE

Broken Hearted

THE LORD IS NEAR TO THOSE WHO HAVE A BROKEN HEART....
—PSALM 34:18

As a parent of a special child, I know what it feels like to have a broken heart. I'm also aware that in this life there are millions of other things that can break your heart. If your heart is happy or calm, you don't even notice it or feel it. Yet, I remember a time when my heart hurt so badly I felt it with every breath I took.

After Caroline's birth and diagnosis, I remember not even being able to taste food for months. Usually I had loved to sing around the house, but I couldn't sing without crying. At the strangest times and for no apparent reason tears would fall. My husband would help explain my behavior by saying, "She just has a high water level." But we both knew what was going on in our lives—our hearts were broken. Thank God, the Lord was near.

People try to help, but truly only God can offer real and true comfort. Even knowing He's there is a comfort you can't really explain. In the middle of the night when your heart is breaking in hospital rooms and in places of rejection, God's presence can comfort you like no other. As you sense His presence, you realize He truly understands. After all, think of what His child endured. There's great comfort in knowing that He has walked all of this before you, and that He's with you now. There's great comfort in knowing that the Creator of the universe cares about what you're going through.

Never forget this: No One understands you better or loves you more than your heavenly Father. He's the One who sent Jesus to heal the brokenhearted—to heal *your* broken heart.

SIXTY

Never Forsaken

I HAVE BEEN YOUNG, AND NOW AM OLD; YET I HAVE NOT SEEN THE RIGHTEOUS FORSAKEN.... —PSALM 37: 25

I guess I should say I've been young and now I'm middle-aged (though I'm not going to claim the old part), and I have not seen the righteous forsaken. One thing for sure, I've lived long enough to have seen God's faithfulness toward His children.

I remember stories of how my great-grandparents were a few of the blessed people to have good jobs during the Great Depression. They knew they were blessed and continually blessed others. People where I grew up would stop me in grocery stores or the beauty shop and tell me what kind people my grandparents were, and how they helped them during some hard times.

I've also listened to my mother and my grandmother tell story after story of how God came through for our family time and time again. Each generation had a trial or tribulation of its own, but none were ever forsaken. They all lived to tell their children of God's goodness. So when the devil comes in and tries to tell you it's over, remind him of the faithfulness of God to all generations.

Tell your children about the miracles of the past, and it will be the anchor for their future. Remind yourself that God always has been faithful as far back as you can see, and He will be faithful into the future where you and I cannot see. We don't need to know where or how God will help us; we just need to know that God is faithful and the righteous will not be forsaken.

SIXTY-ONE

Perfect

THE LORD WILL PERFECT THAT WHICH CONCERNS ME....
—PSALM 138:8

What concerns you today? Whatever it is the Lord said He would perfect it.

And we can trust God to keep His Word because He's not a man that He should lie (Numbers 23:19). He would not promise something if He wouldn't or couldn't plan on doing it.

Most of the time when you hear politicians speak, they're very careful about the promises or commitments they make, knowing the limits of their abilities. Even as a mom, I make it a point to be equally as careful. I rarely say, "Yes, we will go to Wal-Mart this afternoon." I'm much more likely to say, "If everything works out, we'll go to Wal-Mart today." Trust me, I've been a mom a long time now, and I know if I don't keep my word I will have five children immediately reminding me.

I also realize that my abilities are limited especially on certain days. Yet, aren't we glad that God knows His abilities, and they aren't limited at all. He is the only One who can perfect the things that concern you. Actually, He may be the only One who knows *what* concerns you. So by all means, talk to your heavenly Father and tell Him what's on your heart. Then watch Him change details and move circumstances around until it's perfect for you—His child whom He loves.

"Without the assistance of the Divine Being . . . I cannot succeed. With that assistance I cannot fail."
—Abraham Lincoln

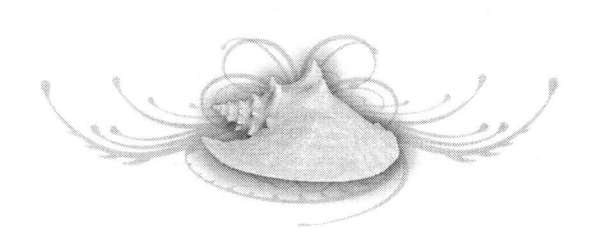

"Life is a daring adventure or nothing."
—Helen Keller

SIXTY-TWO

Family

NO WEAPON FORMED AGAINST YOU SHALL PROSPER, AND EVERY TONGUE WHICH RISES AGAINST YOU IN JUDGMENT YOU SHALL CONDEMN. THIS IS THE HERITAGE OF THE SERVANTS OF THE LORD, AND THEIR RIGHTEOUSNESS IS FROM ME, SAYS THE LORD. — ISAIAH 54:17

Life was pretty exciting in my house while growing up. I was the only girl with four brothers, so there was lots of testosterone in the house. My brothers were more than ready to fight for anything or nothing. If you have boys you will understand.

If anyone came against a member of our family, the person had a fight on his or her hands. This is just the way boys settled things. It really did not matter if the accusations were true or not, the person was still in for a fight. Truly, we were a strong and closely-knit group, and we took things personally as we should have.

Likewise, we are now in God's family, and He takes it personally if any weapon is formed against His family. Aren't we privileged to be in His family?! Trust me, there are benefits!

Isaiah 54 says God will stop any weapons or words that come up against you, and they will not prosper. This is your heritage as part of God's family. God's Word goes on to say that it doesn't matter if these weapons or words are true or not because our righteousness is from Him. Wow! We have His righteousness just because we're in God's family.

When words are used to hurt you or your child, know that they will not prosper for He has promised, and He is faithful. He has surrounded your family—which is His family too—with a shield of protection.

# SIXTY-THREE

Before I Go to Bed

"BE ANGRY, AND DO NOT SIN": DO NOT LET THE SUN GO DOWN ON YOUR WRATH. — EPHESIANS 4: 26

I always remind my children to say their prayers before they go to bed, and they assure me that they always do. But maybe they need to remind their mother to say hers.

It was the last week of school, and everyone knows that week is the hardest. I just happened to be on recess duty when two little boys in trouble were brought to a nearby teacher to be reprimanded.

"Why did you spit on her?" I overheard the teacher asking. At that moment, I realized it was my daughter they were talking about.

As the two little boys faced their teacher realizing how angry she was, God supernaturally gave me the grace to forgive immediately.

But that wasn't good enough for the devil. He waited until late that night when I was exhausted and brought the whole incident before me all over again. As I retold the story to my husband word for word—wow—the madder I got just thinking about it. My husband and I were overwhelmed at the nerve of two healthy boys who would do this to our child. We were firmly resolved to pick up the phone first thing in the morning and call the principal, the boys' parents and even the church's pastor about the boys' behavior. We recounted the event for at least another thirty minutes and concluded that these two boys would probably be a menace to society.

Then we also started remembering all God had forgiven us for and how He hadn't repaid us for our sins. We turned out to be good citizens who love God even though at times in our lives people could have questioned our potential in society. We remembered that we are all a work in progress and in need of a lot of grace. And we remembered what we all did to God's son and how quickly He forgave us.

So by 11:30 that evening and a little more tired, we had come full circle remembering who we are and what we do. We love and live, and each day we have something to forgive because we are God's children, and we act like Him.

Then John and I prayed that God would forgive us, and we would freely forgive others. Yes, we were angry—and most people would agree that we had a right to be. Yet, God helped us not to sin, and by His help we did not let the sun go down on our wrath.

SIXTY-FOUR

Partake

> BELOVED, DO NOT THINK IT STRANGE CONCERNING THE FIERY TRIAL WHICH IS TO TRY YOU…BUT REJOICE TO THE EXTENT THAT YOU PARTAKE OF CHRIST'S SUFFERINGS, THAT WHEN HIS GLORY IS REVEALED, YOU MAY ALSO BE GLAD WITH EXCEEDING JOY.
> —1 PETER 4:12-13

The extent to which you partake in Christ's suffering will determine your joy when His glory is ultimately revealed. Actually, whenever you have a part in something little or big, you feel joy when it's completed.

I recently attended a high school graduation where teachers, students—and for sure, the parents—were moved to tears as they recalled memories from the past years. At this particular school, the tradition was to show pictures comparing each student in kindergarten and then on the day of graduation. It was great to see how the toothless little child turned out to be a strong, beautiful man or woman. As much as I enjoyed it, my joy was small compared to the parents who had seen this child through thirteen years of school.

On that occasion of joy, all the trials endured through all the years seemed so small compared to the joy of the occasion. The same is true where you are concerned. If you refuse to quit, then all of the fiery trials this world puts you through will pale in comparison to the glory that is awaiting all who finish their earthly race.

My experience as a spectator at the graduation affected me to a degree. Yet, there's no comparison to the joy of the graduate's parents. After all, the parents worked, sacrificed and invested their lives into their child all through the years, and now glory had come. What joy!

Give God your best—just as He gave you His best by sending Jesus. And then to the extent to which you partake of Christ will determine your level of joy when He returns.

SIXTY-FIVE

Early Morning Prayer

> NOW IN THE MORNING, HAVING RISEN A LONG WHILE BEFORE DAYLIGHT, HE WENT OUT AND DEPARTED TO A SOLITARY PLACE; AND THERE HE PRAYED. — MARK 1:35

Having mentioned previously the busyness of our household, it should come as no surprise that I've learned the only time to enjoy a quiet moment is early in the morning. I love to get up early with a cup of coffee and my Bible, and let Jesus remind me who I am and that I can make it. Then I'm ready when the hurricane hits, and they all arise.

You see, prayer is like water for a Christian, and we know the Word of God is our food. Matthew 4:4 says that man shall not live by bread alone, but by every word that proceeds from the mouth of God. Yet prayer also is essential to being connected to the vine.

Jesus prayed often and early. He knew that He could not make it without prayer. Even the night He was betrayed, He was found praying in the garden. Before His ministry began, He prayed and fasted for forty days, and He later told the disciples to watch and pray lest they fall into temptation. Jesus believed in prayer.

No wonder. Prayer waters the Word planted in your heart, and through the Word and prayer you will see yourself grow. Areas that used to make you stumble and fall will lose their hold on you.

As parents we have so many responsibilities and so much that must be accomplished every day that we can be tempted to miss a day or two or even a week of prayer. But remember, no one had more to accomplish than Jesus, and He woke up early and went out to pray. Jesus knew He needed to talk to the Father often, and we must also talk to the Father often.

Do you need to get things accomplished every day? Well then, right here is the key: The Scripture says that the effective, fervent prayers of a righteous person avails or accomplishes much.

SIXTY-SIX

Our Rescuer

... HE SAVED THEM OUT OF THEIR DISTRESSES. HE SENT HIS WORD AND HEALED THEM, AND DELIVERED THEM FROM THEIR DESTRUCTIONS. — PSALM 107:19-20

The children of Israel sure got themselves in some messes by removing themselves from God's protective covering. Unfortunately, many of us do the same thing today. So what did God do about it back then? What does He do today?

Did God get mad and turn His back on them? No, He delivered them out of their distresses or problems and so much more. He sent His Word and healed them. And He's done the same thing for you and me.

The Bible says if we sin—or when we sin—we are to confess our sins to the Father, and He is just and faithful and will forgive us. He delivers us and restores what is rightfully ours because we are His children.

When my children were little—and even now as teenagers—they get into some pretty interesting situations. How do I respond? Do I get mad and leave them in whatever mess they have created? No way. I help restore them and put them back on their feet.

God's also in the business of restoring His children. So don't ever let condemnation steal what is rightfully yours; God's help is rightfully yours. Romans 8:1 says, "There is therefore now *no* condemnation to those who are in Christ Jesus." So if you find yourself in a mess, quickly call for your Father's help. Then receive it and all the restoration that goes with it.

We can get pretty banged up down here on Earth. But God was well aware of that fact, which is why He sent a Healer. So run to the mercy seat and find grace and help in time of need. Receive all of God's goodness. I could use the rest of this book to list God's goodness. There's more than enough to go around, and He wants you to have all you need and want.

SIXTY-SEVEN

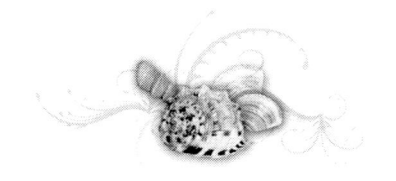

Boasting

> ... "MY GRACE IS SUFFICIENT FOR YOU, FOR MY STRENGTH IS MADE PERFECT IN WEAKNESS." THEREFORE MOST GLADLY I WILL RATHER BOAST IN MY INFIRMITIES, THAT THE POWER OF CHRIST MAY REST UPON ME. —2 CORINTHIANS 12:9

Think about Paul's words for a minute. He said he could actually be glad about his weaknesses since he had great confidence in God's strength that's made perfect in weaknesses. And really, isn't it true that God shows the whole wide world His perfect strength when you feel the weakest?

Notice I said *"feel the weakest,"* but I did not say *"go around proclaiming it."* What we need to go around proclaiming—or boasting—is the fact that God strengthens us in everything He calls us to do. People who live a *"normal"* life (by the way, *normal* is just a setting on a dryer) have no idea of the mountains special parents of special kids must climb. Yet, dear friends, I promise even though you feel weak climbing these mountains, His strength is being perfected in your family. You have God's personal guarantee!

With a large family, all whom have special needs of one kind or the other, I sometimes feel like I'm running a race crippled. I'm tempted to say "no fair!" when I see other families signing up their children for every sport and dropping them off at activities with no thought of whether there will be a place for a special child or if he or she will be accepted.

I understand completely that sometimes as a special parent even the more minor and seemingly mundane things of everyday life can be exhausting physically and emotionally. There are days you're not sure you can make it. But that's also when we can take Paul's words to heart and trust that God's strength—not ours—is made perfect in our weakness. That's quite a divine exchange! We hand over our weakness, and God hands back His strength.

The truth is, no matter how we feel every day and every year we do make it, and we will keep making it. We will enjoy ourselves and boast in Christ's power that rests upon us to do His will. We must purpose to live our lives by supernatural power.

I see in my own family that in many ways we are not weaker—but stronger—because of the mountains we have climbed together. Remember, there can be no testimony without a test. So boast in the fact that the Lord is making you strong!

SIXTY-EIGHT

The Prodigal Son

... THE GOODNESS OF GOD LEADS YOU TO REPENTANCE.
—ROMANS 2:4

Over the years so many folks—even churches—have incorrectly told the story of the prodigal son so that people believe that God allows bad things to happen to people in order to draw them to Christ. That's absolutely not true!

We serve a good God who sent His only Son to die for us so none would perish. The Bible says God is not willing that anyone should perish (2 Peter 3:9). So what happened to the prodigal son? He walked with the thief and that thief, the devil, took all he had.

But let me ask this important question. What drew the prodigal son back to his father? The Bible says that he started remembering how good he had it in his father's house. In a way, he knew the plans and thoughts of his father and knew there was hope for the future. He knew his father was good because he knew his father.

Perhaps you have a stronghold in your mind, thinking that God sent something your way to bring you into right-standing with Him. Let's clear this up right now. That's just *not* how

God works. In fact, Jesus died to be good to you. You are God's child, and He sent Jesus to take away your sin and your sickness. God is reaching out to you the same way the father of the prodigal son reached out to his son. That's the whole point of that Bible example.

World renowned preacher Oral Roberts once said, "When people see God as a good God, they receive their healing." Yet, as long as you feel compelled to pay the price for your sin, you cannot receive the fact that Jesus paid it all.

God *is* a good God.

SIXTY-NINE

This Little Light of Mine

NO ONE, WHEN HE HAS LIT A LAMP, COVERS IT WITH A VESSEL ...
FOR WHOEVER HAS, TO HIM MORE WILL BE GIVEN.... —LUKE 8:16, 18

One of the cutest videos I have is of my special Caroline singing, "This little light of mine, I'm going to let it shine. Let it shine. Let it shine. Let it shine." She is about two years old, and it's so funny as she holds up that little finger letting it shine. But my very favorite part of the song is when she sings, "Don't let Satan blow it out" and puffs. She would blow that finger so hard, those little fat cheeks and cute mouth made everyone laugh.

Truly, babies are such a precious gift from God. We all know that even if we're exhausted and waiting in line at the grocery store and a baby in front smiles, that sparkle in those little eyes makes us remember why we do everything we do. And it's that sparkle that I want to talk about.

God puts that "sparkle" in every child, but the world is constantly trying to blow it out. We've always been very careful about what we've said about all of our children. But

~143~

we've also been watchful—and some would say overly cautious—about the impact others have on them. Yet, it's our responsibility to make sure that Satan doesn't blow out their little lights.

The world uses all kinds of ways to remove that sparkle from your child's eyes—wrong televisions shows, friends, negative teachers and hurtful words from family or friends. Guard the ears and eyes of your child, and don't discuss their problems in front of them as if they don't understand. Everyone, no matter how young, understands negative words.

In verse 18 of Luke, Jesus says to whomever has, more will be given. So if you or someone else lets a light go out, even what they have will be taken away. It seems like once that happens in any child, he or she slips into a downward spiral. It all comes down to this: Negative causes negative, but positive seeds or words produce positive children.

Guard that little light in your child, and watch it grow into something so big the whole world will take note.

SEVENTY

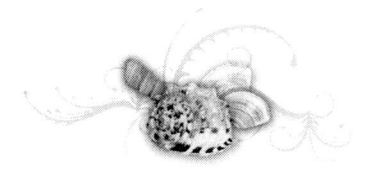

The Lion, the Bear, Oh No

MOREOVER DAVID SAID, "THE LORD, WHO DELIVERED ME FROM THE PAW OF THE LION AND FROM THE PAW OF THE BEAR, HE WILL DELIVER ME FROM THE HAND OF THE PHILISTINE".... —1 SAMUEL 17:37

In this passage David was trying to convince the king that he was able to go against the giant because of his track record of conquering with God's help in the past. David was bold with confidence, and he knew first and foremost that it was God who had delivered him from the lion and the bear. David trusted in God's faithfulness and knew that together they could slay any giant.

It was defeating the lion and the bear that gave David his confidence in God's power. These seemingly scary things actually helped his faith in God develop and grow.

What if David had let the lion or the bear devour his sheep? In that case he wouldn't have witnessed God's great power. He might even have been tempted to fall into self-pity saying, "Well, if it isn't a lion or a bear coming against my family, it's something else. I mean it's always one thing or another." No. David didn't talk that way. David wasn't a coward, and he did not run from the battle. In fact, conquering the lion and the bear prepared him for the giant. And killing the giant created his place in the kingdom.

Look at the lion and the bear in your life as preparation. Let them build your confidence in the Lord. Then, in life's scariest trials you'll run toward the battle like David did—ready to conquer victoriously!

SEVENTY-ONE

Ebenezer

THEN SAMUEL TOOK A STONE AND SET IT UP BETWEEN MIZPAH AND SHEN, AND CALLED ITS NAME EBENEZER, SAYING, "THUS FAR THE LORD HAS HELPED US." —1 SAMUEL 7:12

A battle was on, and the Israelites were surrounded by the Philistines once again. We know from chapters preceding 1 Samuel in the Bible that the Philistines attacked Israel and stole the Ark of the Covenant. Then, in verse 12 above, God's children were threatened again.

But Samuel spoke up! Giving the people hope, he instructed the Israelites to return to the Lord and only serve Him with all their hearts. Samuel told them if they obeyed, God would deliver them.

Sure enough, verse 9 says the Lord answered Samuel and drove back the Philistines. Samuel made a memorial out of stones so all the people would see and remember where and how the Lord had mightily helped them in their journey. He called the place Ebenezer.

Maybe you and I should make some *Ebenezers*. Every time God answers a prayer or helps us in any way, maybe we should make an Ebenezer of it. We should remember the goodness of

God and talk about it, telling our spouses, our children, our friends, our whole family how God came through and delivered us.

Then the next time the devil comes along and tries to tell you that you're defeated or throws up challenges and obstacles in your face, you can remind him of your Ebenezers.

I'll tell you what, when the devil starts pestering me about the impossibilities of the future, I start listing for him all the miracles in my life. Before I'm done with my list, he's nowhere to be found.

So lay a stone and mark your memories with an Ebenezer every time God comes through and delivers you. One day you'll look back over your life and see the long path of stones that helped you finish your race.

SEVENTY-TWO

Perfume

> NOW THANKS BE TO GOD WHO ALWAYS LEADS US TO TRIUMPH IN CHRIST, AND THROUGH US DIFFUSES THE FRAGRANCE OF HIS KNOWLEDGE IN EVERY PLACE. —2 CORINTHIANS 2:14

Smells to a mother are very important. Let's face it, we're always buying candles and cleaning products to rid our lives of the awful smells that come with family life. With five children, and usually a number of pets, you can only imagine some of the smells I've encountered.

I'll never forget the Christmas morning (we had three children in their twos) I went to my son's room and discovered an awfully nasty smell. Following the trail of the scent led me to his closet where I found, to my surprise, that he had an accident in the toy box. So I spent Christmas morning disinfecting an entire toy box full of toys.

Smells also bring to mind a very pleasant childhood memory. When I was a little girl my grandmother had a wealthy friend who always smelled wonderful. I loved to hug her because it was such a delight. Even then, I decided that when I grew up I wanted to smell really good like she did. Still today, perfume is one of my favorite gifts.

Actually, smells lead us to good or bad things in this life. God's Word encourages us to lead people to Jesus Christ by the beautiful fragrance of our lives as Christians. That should be our goal. Unfortunately, I've been around many parents of special children who left me feeling sad because they were so focused on all of the negatives. Others have been like a breath of fresh air.

What kind of fragrance do you want to give off? The knowledge of Jesus Christ is good news, and we should smell good like Him. Determine to smell so good that the sweet fragrance of Christ lingers long in the mind of everyone you meet.

SEVENTY-THREE

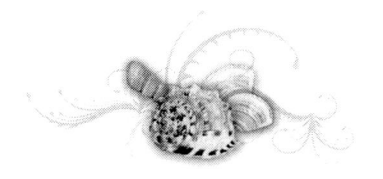

Raising Children

TRAIN UP A CHILD IN THE WAY HE SHOULD GO, AND WHEN HE IS OLD HE WILL NOT DEPART FROM IT. —PROVERBS 22:6

Years ago I became a child of God and what a wonderful Father He has been to me. God is the best example of a parent any of us could have, and our Father has a special weapon. It's the same powerful weapon He used to create everything you and I see. He used this power to create the entire universe, the Earth and everything in it.

What is this power? His *words*. Amazingly enough, we have the same power within us. God creates with His words. In fact, He *always* speaks the way He wants things to be, not the way things are.

As soon as I became a Christian He called me righteous and told me I was in a royal family. He said that I was blessed and highly favored and that I was more than a conqueror even when I failed. In all my mistakes and shortcomings, I've never once heard Him say I was anything less than victorious. I've searched the Scriptures, and I can't find one, single negative word that He's spoken toward His children.

Isn't this how we should raise our children? Of course it is! We should raise them up—train them up—in the way we want them to go or the way we want them to be.

I remember a special education teacher who would play the song "You Raise Me Up" frequently for her class. She used the song to help the special children reach their potential. Yet, isn't this how we should raise *all* children?

We need to continually tell them who they *really* are—who God says they are and what they can accomplish. The world is most definitely telling them who they want them to be, and look around, the children listen. Drown out those other voices of the world and the media, and get in agreement with God and what He says about your children and their lives. Set your child up for success!

I heard a renowned special education leader once say if all your child does well is tighten the screws for you in the house, then you better go loosen all the screws in the house before he or she gets off the school bus. In other words, give them ample occasions to succeed every day.

Make sure your child knows how great he or she is at something! After all, isn't that what God has done for you? Speak those things that are not as though they are (Romans 4), and then watch and see that God's secret weapon of words will cause your child to rise above all the things in this life that tried to push him or her down.

SEVENTY-FOUR

Daily Bread

AND FORGIVE US OUR DEBTS, AS WE FORGIVE OUR DEBTORS.
—MATTHEW 6:12

In the gym working out not long ago, I felt compelled to say the Lord's Prayer aloud for my husband and for me to think about. When I got to this part in verse 12 "forgive us our debts," it leaped in my heart.

Days went on as days always do, and once again John and I were talking (even after twenty years we still enjoy each other's company). Yet, this time it wasn't quite so holy of a conversation. We went down one of those sensitive roads that married couples sometimes travel. This conversation was about someone who had left one of our boys out of an elite little basketball team.

As small as it may sound, it really made me mad. Whenever we see our children hurt, it tends to bring the mama bear out in all of us. Then talking to John, I went on for quite a while on the things I wish the person knew or didn't know. Then, just like our faithful Father, He reminded me of my *daily bread* or that wonderful place of sustenance in Him where I go and receive everything I need.

In that daily place, I ask the Lord to forgive my debts, and He asks me to forgive my debtors. In hearing the prayer this time, I was quickened that we needed daily bread. Of course we do! I mess up daily, so it shouldn't surprise me that other people do, too.

Yet, God is the best at forgiving. He forgave the whole world of its sins and sent one Son to the Cross so none would need to perish. Dear Father, help us to be more like You—*daily.*

SEVENTY-FIVE

Pass It On

> ... HE BLESSED AND BROKE AND GAVE THE LOAVES TO THE DISCIPLES; AND THE DISCIPLES GAVE TO THE MULTITUDES.
> — MATTHEW 14:19

The Word of God is amazing! I've read this Scripture many times, but then one day a new point suddenly leaped out at me.

Jesus was with God from the beginning and helped create the entire universe. He heals the sick, raises the dead and still takes care of you and me. So do you really think in order to feed 5,000 He needed one boy's lunch and help to pass out loaves and fish?

No! He didn't *need* help; He chose help. Jesus could have spoken and instantly watched food for 5,000 appear. Yet, instead, He chose to use a little boy's lunch, and He chose for His disciples to help Him pass out the food.

It's very interesting to me that He wants our help. I believe the whole point is that if we are truly His disciples in this hour, then He's requiring our work in the end-time harvest. In fact, He's asking us to go into the entire world and preach the good news!

Once when our pastor was preaching, I saw a mini-vision of how God intends to reach the whole planet. Briefly, I saw a few drops that looked like water drip from the ceiling of the church. Then I saw water rush from the pulpit to the congregation. This all happened in a brief second, but instantly I knew that was how the whole Earth would be covered with God's glory. The Word comes down from heaven to the pastor and then from the pastor to us. It's up to us to share the good news everywhere to flood the Earth.

You see, I know people and talk to people that our pastor doesn't even know. So it's in my hands to share the gospel with them. When God gives me something that helps me, it's not mine to hide but to give away. Isn't that your job as well?

God is good and His mercy never ends, but the devil is out there continually trying to cover and overshadow God's goodness with lies. The devil tells lies that God makes you sick, or God is mad at the world, or there's no hope for you. Lies. Lies. Lies.

It's the devil who brought sickness to this Earth. God loves the world—so much that He sent His only Son to pay the price so *none* would perish. There's always hope for you—for all—in our wonderful Savior.

So it's up to you and me to pass it on, and God's Word says, "…for the earth shall be full of the knowledge of the Lord as the waters cover the sea" (Isaiah 11:9).

SEVENTY-SIX

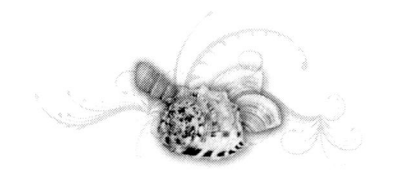

Turn, Turn from Sin and Sorrow

WHEN I KEPT SILENT, MY BONES GREW OLD THROUGH MY GROANING ALL THE DAY LONG. — PSALM 32:3

Repentance is not a feeling or emotion or even a wave of godly quilt. Repentance is a reversal of thought—turning around your way of thinking and behavior. It's a total turnaround!

You see, most people sin or remain in sin because their thinking is wrong. They decided they knew best and did things their way. Actually, they're deceived into thinking their will is better than the will of God.

Yet, God's will is always far better than anything we could think or imagine, and that's why Romans 12:2 says not to be conformed to this world but be transformed. In other words, if you want to live a successful and happy life, change your thinking to line up with the Word. After all, God made You, and He knows what's best for you. The guidelines and instructions He gives you in His Word aren't trying to spoil your good times; He's actually trying to make sure you have good times—a good life.

David was dealing with his covered sin in the text passage. When he kept silent, he even felt age come into his very bones. Whenever I've made a conscious decision to remain in a sin, whether it was not forgiving someone or worry or whatever, I felt bothered and aggravated. And usually, it resulted in me feeling tired and negative. Plain and simple—covered up sin makes you feel old.

But here's the good news: The joy of the Lord is your strength, and with repentance, comes great joy. A few chapters later in the book of Psalms, we see David repent and his life restored. The truth is, hidden sin brings deterioration, but repentance brings life.

Jesus wants us to know the truth and let it set us free (John 8:32). So ask the Lord to reveal His truth in every area of your life (Ephesians 1). Repent. Turn your thinking around. Be free.

SEVENTY-SEVEN

Oh, Be Careful Little Ears What You Hear

AS SOON AS JESUS HEARD THE WORD THAT WAS SPOKEN, HE SAID TO THE RULER OF THE SYNAGOGUE, "DO NOT BE AFRAID; ONLY BELIEVE." — MARK 5:36

I've always thought the joy people get out of telling bad news is strange. I've seen people make a beeline across the church to tell something awful. Here even in Jesus' day, someone pushed through the crowds to tell Jairus the worst news a father could possibly hear.

This time Jesus overheard the gossip (or does He hear every time?), and it caused Him to stop and respond. Jairus, a ruler in the church of that day, knew where he could find help for his sick daughter, and he knew that Jesus recognized faith. He found Jesus and told Him about his little girl so Jesus started on His way to help.

But as Jesus was on His way to pray for the daughter, He met a desperate woman who touched the hem of His garment.

I'm so glad Jesus stops for desperate women. In the middle of this great miracle for Jairus' little daughter, which would do nothing but increase your faith, someone comes running up with bad news. It would be like a pitcher of cold water on a roaring fire.

As it turned out, some people who had come from Jairus' house said the little girl had died and suggested Jairus not trouble the Master anymore. I can identify with Jairus, can't you? It reminds me of times I've been in the Word or at a church meeting, and it seemed as though I was so full of faith that I had wings to fly. Then, the first person you run into shoots you down.

Well, listen to what Jesus said to the father because He's still saying it today: "Don't be afraid! Only believe!" Yes, that's exactly what Jesus is saying to you today!

Fear is the exact opposite of faith, and Jairus, the ruler of the synagogue, was surrounded with cynical unbelievers every day. So what was he to do—give up and believe his peers or believe Jesus? Thank God he listened to Jesus.

Jesus came into the house, told the dead girl to arise, and she did. Remember Jesus only speaks the truth, and He said all things are possible. But you must fear not and only believe. If Jesus tarries—oh, be careful little ears what you hear.

SEVENTY-EIGHT

The Content of the Heart

BUT THE LORD SAID TO SAMUEL, "DO NOT LOOK AT HIS APPEARANCE OR AT HIS PHYSICAL STATURE, BECAUSE I HAVE REFUSED HIM. FOR THE LORD DOES NOT SEE AS A MAN SEES; FOR MAN LOOKS AT THE OUTWARD APPEARANCE, BUT THE LORD LOOKS AT THE HEART." —1 SAMUEL 16:7

The presidential election of 2008 made a great mark on our nation's history. Our great country elected our first African-American president, and I believe it's really long overdue.

Earlier in my career, I had the wonderful opportunity of teaching in an all-black school and saw firsthand what many African Americans had to overcome. Many, many wonderful African Americans in our country have done just that—overcome.

I loved hearing the famous Martin Luther King Jr. speak. The greatest passion comes from suffering and the passion in his voice was beyond inspiring. To me one of the greatest parts of his "I Have a Dream" speech is when he says he has a dream that his four children would one day live in a nation where they will not be judged by the color of their skin, but by the content of their character.

I also have a dream that my five children will experience a nation that does not judge people by their looks or abilities, but looks deeper and sees the heart. That is what God was trying to get Samuel to understand all these years ago. David was a small, red-haired boy who naturally speaking was nothing to write home about. But what Samuel couldn't see was that David would become a leader with incomparable courage and passion that would change Israel forever.

Many times with my own children or my third-grade class, I look in their eyes and remind myself that I don't know who this little student may be one day. Many even seemingly average little students rise to be great.

As troubling as it is, in the weakness of human nature, we often equate ability and potential with only what we see, forgetting that what is in the heart is far stronger. Even more troubling, Hollywood has spent millions of dollars to convince society that appearance is solely how we value people. This has proven to be very damaging to us all. It's not just a travesty for the weak or handicapped, but to all our young sons and daughters who feel valued only if they match the glamorous images they see on television.

So I have a dream as well: that we as a nation—and personally—will turn the tide away from judging people by outward appearances. Outward things are of no consequence because they fade or change. But we must be determined to recognize that the heart of a person is far more precious than what any of us can see. After all, it's the heart that counts.

SEVENTY-NINE

To All Generations

FOR THE LORD IS GOOD; HIS MERCY IS EVERLASTING, AND HIS TRUTH ENDURES TO ALL GENERATIONS. — PSALM 100:5

Sitting here on a sunny Sunday afternoon, I feel the Lord's goodness all around. My five children and a few of the neighborhood kids are running in and out the back door, the men are at the back fence sharing stories as they try once again to fix the fence the children keep breaking. And here I sit with my Bible and a glass of iced tea—blessed to be right in the middle of the wonderful place I call my life.

I remember watching my grandmother and my mother sit down on Sunday and just rest. They both played the piano for church and a great relief came every Sunday when they were done. I'm as sure as I sit here that my children and their children also will one day sit and enjoy this same wonderful peace. One thing you can count on is that the Lord is good and His mercy continues to all our generations. That in itself is worth shouting about.

So refuse to worry today! Know that the Lord is good, and He will continue to be good to all of your children. His goodness and truth never end and certainly are not limited to only some of your children or to one generation. God is good and the truth of that goodness will endure for all generations. So rest in knowing that He delights in being good to you and to your children forever and always.

EIGHTY

Forget About Yourself

DO NOT MERELY LOOK OUT FOR YOUR OWN PERSONAL INTERESTS, BUT ALSO FOR THE INTERESTS OF OTHERS. — PHILIPPIANS 2:4 *(NAS)*

People are the most like Jesus when they're devoted to seeing someone else be successful. Think about that for a minute. Think of the extent of all Jesus went through to make us successful.

Jesus left a position of royalty in heaven and came to Earth where the devil ruled, and He knew full well the price He would have to pay for our freedom. I'm always impressed with the young boys who leave all behind in order to cross oceans and sacrifice everything for the freedoms we enjoy in the United States of America.

Having a special child, I've been blessed to meet some of the greatest people in this world—talented individuals who give their best every day to help these little children—not to mention their moms—feel better about themselves.

Caroline at a very young age needed glasses, and every time we'd get the diagnosis we'd feel a little pain in our hearts. But soon after receiving the prescription, we were always ushered next door to the place where we would pick out our glasses. The two kind people who ran the store were Kim and Fred, and I hope I never forget their names.

"Caroline!" they'd holler out, "Where in the world have you been?" Then they'd go on to make the biggest deal of how cute she looked in her new glasses. Somehow, in the middle of us wiping away tears, their sweetness and humor were used by God to bring joy back again.

So whether your job is serving as a soldier in Iraq or selling eye glass frames, do your job with the intent to make life better for someone else. Do your job so that others receive more just by being around you. *Then*, you'll be doing your job like Jesus.

EIGHTY-ONE

Thirsty?

AS THE DEER PANTS FOR THE WATER BROOKS, SO PANTS MY SOUL FOR YOU, O GOD. — PSALM 42: 1

My husband loves to hunt and put his deer stands around or near water because the deer will always seek out the water streams. They will even risk their lives at times to get a drink, and that is how thirsty for God we must be.

When I work out, the only thing I really want when I finish is a big glass of water. I love iced tea, but when you're really thirsty only water will do.

Even in the course of living life, we all naturally get thirsty, but we're continually busy so we settle for pop, tea or whatever we can get in a hurry. That may work for a short time, but if we continue to drink anything and everything but water, our bodies eventually will pay the price for those choices.

Bottom line, your body needs large amounts of water every day, and you need to take the time to drink it. It's proven that you can live a few weeks without food, but you can only survive a few days without water.

In the same way, our spirit needs God to survive. We need to take the time to drink in the Holy Spirit for our survival and welfare. We must deliberately take a drink every day. When you go outside on a really hot day, you take water along to keep hydrated. Likewise, if you're going to be busy on a given day, make provisions to take your spiritual drink as well. Just like you grab a water bottle, grab a teaching CD or music that can fill you up on your way to work or to run errands.

You may think that taking a drink from an interesting talk show or a chapter from the latest self-help book will refresh and hydrate you, but not so. The same way you would hurt yourself naturally by only drinking tea and pop, you'll hurt yourself spiritually if you don't drink the things of God.

As the deer pants for the water, so you and I need to drink of God every day! You won't survive well without it.

EIGHTY-TWO

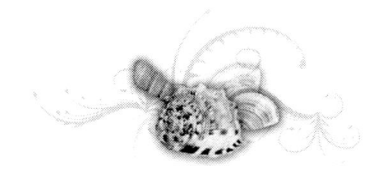

Forever Friends

A FRIEND LOVES AT ALL TIMES.... —PROVERB 17:17

Many times as moms we tend to forget about ourselves. Instead, we usually focus on the children—basketball and cheerleading and lunches and piano lessons and soccer. Really, we all know the list goes on and on, and that's only part of the list. We also have parents, brothers, sisters, in-laws, aunts, uncles and on and on. Yet, it seems like everyone in that family list is either older or younger, and everyone of them has his or her own point of view.

So thank God for friends—the ones you've had for years and the ones who are new. Isn't it a blessing to talk and share with someone your own age?

A friend usually is going through the same kind of things you're going through and listens without judging. God sends friends because we couldn't make it many times without the help or encouragement of a friend. Remember that—and don't be tempted to isolate yourself. We are the *body* of Christ, but we cannot function to full capacity alone. Sometimes just laughing with a friend about your teenager or the house that won't stay clean is a priceless experience that the devil would just as soon you not have. The devil isn't for anything that paves the way to a better life for us.

"Forever friends" is how my best friend and I would always sign notes when passing them in class. Through life we have had times when we could spend much time together and then times when we were so busy we rarely saw each other. But we have remained friends for more than thirty years, and through laughter or tears, she always knows what to say. I know God sent her into my life as a gift. I truly love her and know she has always loved me. Thank God for these forever friends.

Pure and simple, true friends—godly friends—are a treasure that God meant for us to enjoy. Pick up the phone, put pen in hand, e-mail or text, but say hello to a friend today!

EIGHTY-THREE

Afraid of the Dark

PERFECT LOVE CAST OUT FEAR.... —1 JOHN 4:18

Not long ago we dealt with a child who was afraid of the dark. No amount of reasoning seemed to help. Even our son sensed his fear was irrational, but he simply did not know how to handle it.

We talked about how there was no need for fear, but that didn't do it. We left lights on, and that didn't seem to help. He tried sleeping in a room with his older brother, but still, he really didn't feel comforted. Intellectually he realized there was nothing to fear, nothing there. But still the fear hung on. The bottom line on fear is that it simply deals in real perceptions and emotions.

Finally in exhaustion, we resorted to the same solution many of you also have tried; we let him lay down in our bed. In a matter of seconds, he was sound asleep. Perfect love. Simply being near the two people on Earth that he knew loved him perfectly quickly chased out all his fears.

Likewise, as God's children when we feel fear gripping us, we need to run as quickly as we can and get as close to our heavenly Father as we can. In those times where fear tries to hang on us, we need to be still and know that He is God. All the irrational fears will leave in a matter of seconds.

"I<small>F YOU WOULD BE
LOVED, LOVE AND
BE LOVABLE.</small>"
—*Benjamin Franklin*

"Y<small>OU CAN GIVE
WITHOUT LOVING,
BUT YOU CANNOT LOVE
WITHOUT GIVING.</small>"
—*Amy Carmichael*

EIGHTY-FOUR

Happily Ever After

IN HOPE OF ETERNAL LIFE WHICH GOD, WHO CANNOT LIE, PROMISED BEFORE TIME BEGAN. —TITUS 1:2

My son was greatly surprised the other day that all movies don't have happy endings. Watching a movie he said, "Well, you know the dog will run away, and then he'll be back because movies always have to have a happy ending." He felt quite sure of himself because all he's ever seen are children's movies where that *is* how they typically end.

Yet, as we grow up, we begin experiencing life's good times and bad times and bittersweet times. We begin to see life differently. If we're not careful, we almost expect bad things to come our way more than good things to come our way. As adults we can be so fixated and prepared for the worst that in a sense we mentally welcome it.

But for Christians that won't do. We need to be more like children who believe in the end everything will turn out all right. To the world this may seem immature or silly, but we Christians have read the end of *The Book*. We're on the winning side, and we have God's Word on it.

So no matter what you're going through, you're *going through it*. It will come to pass! We're promised all through the Bible that we will spend eternity with our Savior, and we're also promised no tears in heaven. In a sense we've longed for that since we were little children looking for a happily ever after. Yet, a happily ever after is what God really, truly has planned for all His children. Become as a child again and know that in the end, you'll hear, "And they lived happily ever after…for eternity."

EIGHTY-FIVE

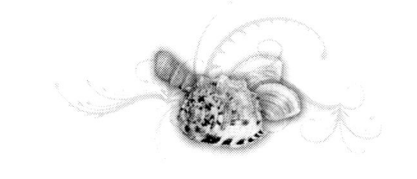

Fear Not

> THEN THE ANGEL SAID TO THEM, "DO NOT BE AFRAID, FOR BEHOLD, I BRING YOU GOOD TIDINGS OF GREAT JOY WHICH WILL BE TO ALL PEOPLE. —LUKE 2:10

Angels came to deliver the greatest news the Earth had ever heard, and yet, what were their very first words? *Fear not!* Those words are still pretty important today.

God created the Earth out of faith, but when the devil entered the Earth he brought fear along with him, and mankind has been dealing with it ever since. Fear is the one thing that can stop you from living in the realm of God's best.

But God sent Jesus to the rescue. Jesus came to Earth to bring goods new to all people for all generations. The Bible says the devil comes to steal, kill and destroy, but Jesus comes to give us—that's you and me—abundant life. In other words, Jesus came to give us the good life! He paid the price for your sins, your sickness and your peace of mind (Isaiah 53:4-5). He's redeemed you from the curse of the law that came upon man when Adam sinned (Galatians 3:13). The curse is no more.

So why would you allow a little thing like fear to keep you from all the good that Jesus brought down here for you?

Sure the devil tries to tell you that you'll fail. But God's Word says you're more than a conqueror (Romans 8:37). Are you fearful of sickness? Acts 10:38 says God anointed Jesus of Nazareth who went about doing good and healing all who were sick and oppressed. Afraid of not having money? Philippians 4:19 says God will meet all your needs according to His riches in glory by Christ Jesus. Maybe you fear that you will once again bring shame upon yourself. But Isaiah 54:4 says you will not suffer the former shame. Let's face it, it doesn't matter what fear the devil throws at you; it's simply one of his devices to distract you from God's goodness.

Fear depletes joy so never let fear enter your life and steal your joy. Jesus died that you might have life and life abundantly, so don't settle for anything less.

Fear not!

EIGHTY-SIX

Follow

... FOLLOW ME, AND I WILL MAKE YOU FISHERS OF MEN.
—MATTHEW 4:19

This morning, walking into my bathroom, I once again tripped over Ralphie, our adorable little dog who loves to go with me everywhere. The only problem with Ralphie is that he doesn't follow so well—he'd rather walk just a little ahead of me and anticipate where he thinks I might be headed. Frankly, his method is not only silly, but it also has proven to be dangerous. Little Ralphie has even bumped and smacked into things because he was so busy looking *backward* to see which room I was entering next.

So on this particular morning I offered Ralphie some good advice. "Ralph," I said in my best motherly voice, "Why don't you just *follow*? It would be easier!"

And then I heard that wonderful shepherd's voice speak in my heart and say, "Why don't *you* just follow?"

Immediately I realized, *Yes! I love God, and yes, I want to be with Him everywhere.* But, I too, have an awful habit of running ahead. I'm the kind of person who's always wondering about tomorrow, or I'm trying to figure out the next move the Holy Spirit is leading us into instead of simply following.

Frankly, my method is not only kind of crazy, but also it may be dangerous.

While I'm busy looking back analyzing every move I often do get hurt. Have you done that too? Yet, Jesus promised that if we would follow Him, that He would make us fisher of men. We need to realize that we are His sheep, we do recognize His voice, and we can follow and not guess our way through life. My heart's desire—and I'm sure yours—is to be with our Master *and* follow Him.

Thanks, Ralph, for such a great lesson.

EIGHTY-SEVEN

Anchors Away

THIS HOPE WE HAVE AS AN ANCHOR OF THE SOUL, BOTH SURE AND STEADFAST, AND WHICH ENTERS THE PRESENCE BEHIND THE VEIL. —HEBREWS 6:19

The ocean is one of my favorite places on Earth. In fact, after graduating from college, I went on a cruise to the Bahamas so I could enjoy the water for days. Even better, I met my wonderful husband on the cruise.

As much as I love the water, I was overwhelmed by its vastness, which is not surprising considering I grew up in Oklahoma. After sailing for only a day, there was no land insight at all. Even though the ocean is beautiful, the perspective from a ship still can be intimidating. The waves of the sea are so strong that a person could be tossed about or become totally lost.

That's why people who sail or go on a cruise develop great respect for the captain and his nautical skills. But did you know that the *anchor holds* an equally important role? (No pun intended.) Without both the captain and the anchor, some people would be lost at sea.

It's the same way in the life of a Christian. The ways of the world can well up around you like waves on the ocean, and without our Captain and our anchor we'd be tossed to and fro. Problems, sickness, debt or confusion of any kind all can seem as vast as the ocean or as overwhelming as a single wave.

But rest easy! Your Captain Jesus is in the boat with you, and you have a hope that anchors your soul both sure and steadfast. Bon voyage!

EIGHTY-EIGHT

Keep Paddling

WHEN YOU PASS THROUGH THE WATERS, I WILL BE WITH YOU;
AND THROUGH THE RIVERS, THEY SHALL NOT OVERFLOW YOU....
— ISAIAH 43:2

I woke up at 5:30 one morning, and before I poured my first cup of coffee the flood of things I needed to do during the day almost took my breath away. I know the world would describe this feeling as an anxiety attack or panic attack, but I believe most adults and probably some children have all experienced this from time to time. I'm sure you've experienced the same feeling I had this morning.

My mind was absolutely flooded. I began to mentally outline my children's day and activities, everything I had to do for my class and to organize in teaching, and on top of it all administrators at my school had asked me to start a special education program. This list doesn't even begin to mention my husband, home, finances and everything else that made the list run on and on and on. The more I thought about it all, the more overwhelmed I became.

But, praise God, when the devil comes in like a flood, God promises to raise a standard against him!

As I poured my morning coffee and sat down with my Bible for devotions, I literally pictured myself like a little dog caught in a large current and paddling with all its might just to keep his head above the fast-moving water. (Thank You, Jesus, that we can sit down to read our Bibles instead of some book on anxiety!) God is so faithful because He caused my eyes to fall immediately on Isaiah 43:2, which says, "When you pass through the waters, I will be with you" (NAS). Hallelujah! I will *pass through* because He is with me. The Scripture goes on to say the waters will not overflow us—we will make it.

You may feel overwhelmed at times, but never forget that our Savior is with you. He knew there would be times like this in life, but He also wants you to remember that He overcame the world.

EIGHTY-NINE

The Word Causes Us to Grow

AND JESUS GREW IN WISDOM AND STATURE.... —LUKE 2:52 *(NIV)*

As the parent of a child who has been diagnosed with Down syndrome, I've read all the medical books, all the self-help books and heard all the negative reports. The truth is, if we aren't careful, we'll let these findings—this wealth of natural information—be held in higher authority than the Word of God. Yet, we must refuse to let that happen; God's Word *must be* our final authority.

One of the many symptoms of Down syndrome is short stature. At first I thought since I'm quite tall, I didn't really care if my daughter was short. After all, I thought she was so cute that it wouldn't matter, but as she got older the Lord helped me see that this was just something that was being stolen from her. And I believe she is entitled to everything that is rightfully hers. I decided I simply did not want this diagnosis to reign in her body—not to mention she loves to play basketball. That's really where this issue all began.

A few years ago, Caroline was measured for stats to be printed on her basketball picture trading cards, and she was four feet eight inches, which is a little short for her age. So I began speaking God's Word over the situation. After all, there's power in God's Word—whether I speak or He does. We have God's promise that His Word does not return void (Isaiah 55:11). I spoke the Word and spoke the Word over Caroline, confessing that she would grow in wisdom and in stature. Two years later, while being measured for her basketball pictures, we realized just how much she had grown. She had grown to five feet tall, not bad at all for a sixth-grader.

The Word of God is powerful and causes us to grow inside and out. Find the Scripture you need for the very symptom or situation in your life. Then keep applying it, and watch the Word change your life.

NINETY

A Helping Hand

IT IS GOD HIMSELF WHO HAS MADE US WHAT WE ARE AND GIVEN US NEW LIVES FROM CHRIST JESUS; AND LONG AGES AGO HE PLANNED THAT WE SHOULD SPEND THESE LIVES IN HELPING OTHERS. — EPHESIANS 2:10 (TLB)

One afternoon I began reading this verse, and it inspired great expectations in my heart. The verse begins explaining that God Himself made us what we are and gives us a new life. The excitement continued to build in me when I read the next words, which said, *"He planned it long ago."* Wow! That hit me. I was getting ready and being prepared for whatever great thing He planned a long time ago that I would do.

Then, there were those seven profound little words: *"We should spend our lives helping others."* To be honest, I was a little shocked. I thought for sure the verse would mention how He planned us for some sort of greatness or great purpose.

But think about those words for a minute; I thought about them for quite a while. The Scripture isn't simply saying that we should go on an occasional mission's trip or teach a Sunday school class. No! This Scripture is saying that we should spend our lives helping others. That's not one "helping"—that's a whole lifetime of helping.

Then it hit me. That's the kind of life Jesus invested in us. He spent His whole life helping people—teaching, preaching, healing, giving and loving everyone He met.

Can you even imagine what the world would be like if we all spent our lives helping others like Jesus did?

Most people in this world are only concerned about getting what they want and going where they want to go. Yet, God has a whole different plan for your life, and amazingly enough, His plan will make your life a whole lot happier.

I dare you for a week—or as long as you can—to be continually on the look out for someone in need of a helping hand. Take the time while working, shopping—even ministering—to see whom you can help.

I had the privilege recently to work with a precious teacher who had taught for many years, but was hit with cancer. She was a great lady before getting sick and even greater while she was sick. I really don't know how, but even through all kinds of treatments she rarely missed school. And she didn't just show up at school, she came in and brightened the room. Even when she felt awful, she never used it for an excuse to give less of herself.

In fact, I hope I never forget the day I once again got stuck entering my grades into our computer system, but like always, she stopped and reached over me with her little, thin arms and gave me a helping hand. I knew this woman for years and that is the way she always was—helping others. But not until her funeral did I hear even more stories of her faithfulness. I was very sad to see her go, but I was so encouraged to have seen firsthand a woman who truly spent her life helping others.

NINETY-ONE

'Mama'

FOR YOU DID NOT RECEIVE THE SPIRIT OF BONDAGE AGAIN TO FEAR, BUT YOU RECEIVED THE SPIRIT OF ADOPTION BY WHOM WE CRY OUT, "ABBA, FATHER." — ROMANS 8:15

During a recent winter, we experienced one of those blessed days where everything was canceled because of snow. Everything outside was painted white with freshly fallen snow, and it seemed like the activity of the outside world was as frozen as the ground. Those are wonderful days with your family, and of course, too much food.

Our five children were bundled up and outside playing, and David, the baby of the family, opened the back door and simply called, "Mama." I got the greatest sense of delight from that single word in that single moment. I smiled to myself and truly loved what I had heard.

What a complete honor and joy to be a parent. I had to wait a few years and endure a few trials before that privilege was mine, but then God opened the windows of heaven and poured out a blessing that at times we literally don't have room enough to contain. I laugh as I think about my brood of five plus two adults and a dog! Yet, being a mother has been one of the most amazing things I've ever done.

Even more, think about what God endured to receive us as children. Really, no birth pains can compare. God's Word says we have been freed from bondage and He adopted us. Yes, all that so we might be His children. I'm convinced that God considers it a joy and an honor to call us His children. If you had a hard time with that concept, remember the honor you feel when you see your child simply walk into the room. Then imagine the even more infinite love our heavenly Father has for us! There's nothing you could do to lose God's love for you. So call out "Daddy," and make His heart leap.

NINETY-TWO

He Directs

IT IS GOD WHO DIRECTS THE LIVES OF HIS CREATURES: EVERYONE'S LIFE IS IN HIS POWER. — JOB 12:10 (TEV)

Our lives are in God's power. He directs us, and the more we learn to listen, the more we receive goodness from Him.

My special child—or should I say one of my special children—(we are all special in His sight) loves art. Caroline was able to paint with my sister-in-law recently, who's an artist. Caroline loves to spend time that way. In fact, no amount of time ever seems like enough. No matter how long Caroline is there, she wants to stay longer or make plans for the next time.

In fact, Caroline loves painting and drawing any art-related subject. I think she's gifted in this area, but I also believe she enjoys art because it's an expression that people don't feel comfortable judging. There's really no right or wrong—it's a true expression of what you want it to be. No matter how you look at it, Caroline loves art and can't seem to get enough.

One week she was pretty frustrated with school, and John and I began praying that her day would be fashioned perfectly for her. Interestingly enough, a morning or two later I ran into the middle-school art teacher in the school hallway. I'd never spoken to her before about any of Caroline's likes or preferences, yet she began asking me about Caroline's school day and how she spent it.

Actually, our school building is pretty big so running into this teacher and ending up in this conversation was completely God. I do believe it had been supernaturally arranged. Ultimately during our conversation, the teacher asked if Caroline would like to come to her art class every day. I almost couldn't believe what I heard, and I almost cried. I was totally overwhelmed at the goodness of God. He is the One who directed this teacher's path to cross mine in order to give Caroline one of the joys of her heart. Truly, every life is in God's power, and He directs all of us. And Caroline is enjoying art every day because she is His.

NINETY-THREE

Examine

> ... LET US TEST AND EXAMINE OUR WAYS. LET US TURN BACK TO THE LORD. — LAMENTATIONS 3:40 (NLT)

As a teacher I know the only way to really know if a student has learned the lesson is to give a test. As a student I didn't like tests, but as a teacher I find them very beneficial.

Even in our jobs in life we're tested by our bosses. A boss may ask you to give an account of your sales or he may ask you to evaluate yourself in some situation. Actually, God is making that same request of each of us.

The other day I had corrected one of my children, and at that moment I was trying to get that child to do the right thing because we all know two wrongs don't make a right. Yet, in trying to motivate the child, I cut the child down with my words. The very second those words came out of my mouth, I realized they were wrong. I didn't like myself for saying them, but I didn't correct them either.

Thank the Lord for the Holy Spirit. The very next morning that situation was the first thing the Holy Spirit brought to my mind. I thought it over and realized I hadn't passed the test so I repented. Hopefully, I'll pass the exam. We're all still in school in some ways, and the Lord is teaching us. He, more than anyone, wants us to grow and learn so we will become like His precious Son.

"Always bear in mind that your own resolution to succeed is more important than any one thing."
—*Abraham Lincoln*

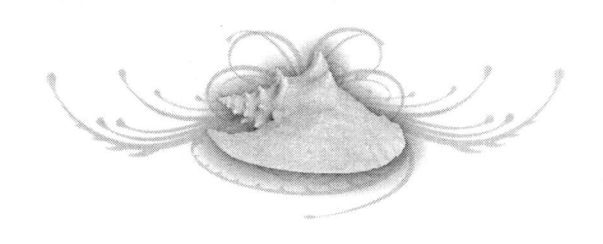

"Self pity is our worst enemy and if we yield to it, we can never do anything good in the world."
—*Helen Keller*

NINETY-FOUR

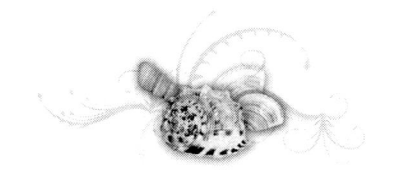

Start Early

NOTHING COULD MAKE ME HAPPIER THAN GETTING REPORTS THAT MY CHILDREN CONTINUE DILIGENTLY IN THE WAY OF TRUTH!—3 JOHN 1:1 *THE MESSAGE*

My new birth to become a Christian was amazing. I instantly saw that all those I thought were against me were really for me. Light became obvious, and the dark became very clear. I felt that I could see as clearly as I would ever need to see. Yet, to my surprise, I soon realized that as we continue walking on in the things of God, every new little area of darkness also will be exposed.

The verses surrounding our text say that if you are a disciple, you will continue in God's Word. Then you'll know the truth, and it will set you free. Think about that for a minute. That means we gradually walk into complete freedom. In other words, the more truth you know, the more you'll be able to recognize lies in your own thinking.

I was born again while I was in high school, and now thirty years later the Lord is still exposing strongholds in my mind. I've wondered, *How did all these strongholds get here?* I'll tell you how! From the time a person is very young, the devil is busy sowing lies of all kinds into a person's mind. He sows strongholds of fear, foolishness, laziness, mediocrity, sickness and depression; the list goes on and on.

Children and adults alike need to confront these lies with the Word of God and meet them head on with the truth. As parents we need to expose wrong thinking patterns in our children every bit as much as we focus on wrong behavior. Attitudes and thinking patterns are critical, and actually, they determine behavior. For instance, if your child doesn't like what is happening in a situation, don't let him or her whine and complain. Teach your children that the Bible says, "In everything give thanks…." Or, if your child is tempted to hold a grudge toward a friend, explain to him or her that Jesus forgave all of us while we were yet sinners, and the Bible asks each one of us to do the same.

Tear down the lies and strongholds the devil is continually trying to build in your child's mind. Remind your child daily that he or she has the mind of Christ. This will require you and your child to know the Word of God which is to grow in truth. That's a good thing. After all, it's never too early to walk in the truth and be set free by its power!

NINETY-FIVE

Write It Down

AT THE LORD'S DIRECTION, MOSES KEPT A WRITTEN RECORD OF THEIR [THE ISRAELITES] PROGRESS.... —NUMBERS 33:2 *(NLT)*

The Lord told me years ago to write down the vision. At times I would be very faithful, but at other times I'd slip up. Looking back, I realize what would happen is that my feelings would rule. Subconsciously I'd decide I didn't have the kind of profound thoughts that needed to be written down.

But I've learned that the whole point isn't how profound our thoughts are, the whole point is the greatness of God! Listen to how the Bible explains it. Psalm 102:18 says, "Write down for the coming generations what the Lord has done, so that people not yet born will praise Him." You see, obeying—and writing down the vision—has everything to do with bringing honor to the works God has done in your life. It's not about you—it's about Him!

When my special Caroline was first born, I really was hanging on by a string emotionally. I began to read Dale Evans' books about her experiences with God and her special child, and it encouraged me so. Her story meant so much to me that if I just saw a picture of their family, I felt lifted up and helped.

These many years later I've come to realize that the Lord has done so many wonderful things in my life that I have to write them down if for no other reason than for my own children to recognize God is faithful to all generations. Truly, as we take pen in hand and write of God's goodness, God will be glorified to this generation and those to come.

NINETY-SIX

Wish or Work

THEREFORE, MY BELOVED BRETHREN, BE STEADFAST, IMMOVABLE, ALWAYS ABOUNDING IN THE WORK OF THE LORD, KNOWING THAT YOUR LABOR IS NOT IN VAIN IN THE LORD.
—1 CORINTHIANS 15:58

When I was young I loved the song "When You Wish upon a Star," and I spent many hours singing and wishing while on the front porch swing. As fun as that may have been, it really didn't accomplish much.

The truth is, wishing is similar to worrying. It keeps your mind very active, but doesn't really change anything or help anything. Don't get me wrong, creative thinking is directly from God. He is the Creator, and we are created in His image to imagine and create. No one is more creative than God, and we should definitely follow in His footsteps.

Yet, notice He didn't just *think creatively*—He set out and actually created. Genesis says that God worked for six days then rested. That's it in a nutshell: There's too much wishing and not enough creative follow-through. If every good idea was acted upon, I'm convinced the world would be a different place.

With special children, or any child, the Lord will lead you and teach you about how to train them. But after He gives you the idea or solution, you are the one who must set that motion into action. Don't be surprised if it takes some work and some time. Nevertheless, if you keep on believing (and working) as the song so sweetly says, you will see your dream come true.

Many times I want to wish that ideas or goals are already accomplished or that things are better than they are. However, in reality, I can wish all day long, but until I get up and do it nothing changes. Using a popular slogan: Just do it!

You see, whether you must repeat the same words for the hundredth time or show your children to tie their shoes every day for what seems like an eternity, your labor is not in vain. You will receive a harvest if you faint not. So wish or work—that is the question. I choose to work and see my wish come true.

NINETY-SEVEN

Friction

AS IRON SHARPENS IRON, SO A MAN SHARPENS THE COUNTENANCE OF HIS FRIEND. — PROVERBS 27:17

I just don't like confrontation or even disagreements. I never have and I never will. One thing I've spent my life doing is avoiding friction. In fact, I've classified myself as a separatist not a puritan.

I've simply believed that if I didn't agree with someone, I'd just separate myself. Actually, it works in some cases. I used to really believe it was the best way to deal with things in a Christian manner. I was convinced my way of thinking was correct.

Then I had a special little child and saw things differently. Suddenly, my eyes were opened to a whole new area in the world and in the church where *someone* needed to wise up and speak up. Maybe to your surprise, it still hadn't dawned on me that "someone" might be me. I still didn't speak up on most occasions. I believed the Lord wanted me to learn not to be offended and assumed that was my lesson to learn.

Friction had actually served me well. Friction? Yes! Anytime one object rubs another, there's friction. That means there's even friction when somebody's attitude rubs you the wrong way. Yet, it can be a good thing because as our text says,

"As iron sharpens iron, so a man sharpens the countenance of his friend."

The real test came as I became the new special education teacher at the largest Christian school in the state of Oklahoma. There have been many new opportunities to inform students and teachers alike about how to recognize, accommodate and be compassionate toward differences and challenges that exist for some in this world. Clearly, it was up to me to do it, and there was no room for excuses any more.

The first day I had to confront some injustices, I wanted to run. I recognize that many people live for occasions to confront, but I am not one of them. I couldn't wait to get home and share my day with my husband. For many people, the incidents might not seem that overwhelming, but they were overwhelming enough to me. I just didn't want to do it.

Then I came across the text Scripture "iron sharpens iron." I realized that movement always causes friction, and movement is what I'd prayed about for many years. The reality is that anytime there's progress in society or personal life, friction is the result. Friction may be uncomfortable at times, but it is nevertheless necessary. It's necessary in order for us to move from glory to glory as God intended.

I've come to realize that if you or I draw back, we will not be shaped into that which God has intended for us to be. If we don't speak the truth in love to our friends, family and co-workers, they won't be shaped into what God desires for them either. Remember, we are His body prepared for good works, so we must work together to become better—even if that means a little friction along the way.

NINETY-EIGHT

See

> ... BECAUSE I SAID TO YOU, 'I SAW YOU UNDER THE FIG TREE,' DO YOU BELIEVE? YOU WILL SEE GREATER THINGS THAN THESE.
> —JOHN 1:50

Many Christians realize that speaking or confessing is a big part of receiving by faith, but the Lord has begun showing me that *seeing* is also a part of receiving.

You may not even realize that seeing plays a role in receiving because perhaps all you've read or heard about your diagnosis or mountain of circumstances has painted a certain picture in your mind of the future. Unfortunately, maybe the diagnosis or the challenges have painted a negative future picture.

But let me tell you this. If your picture doesn't line up with God's Word, then it needs to go. It needs to be repainted with the truth of God's Word. Let me encourage you to get into God's Word and *see* what God has in store for your child. Begin seeing the hope and the good future that's been promised to you in Jeremiah 29:11.

See greater things than you've seen in the past. Don't limit God in what you see or how you pray, but *see* good success! Do you actually believe Jesus when He said that you will see greater things than you have?

A few years ago, I found myself seeing the very least for my special baby. The only thing I compared was the negative future I saw for her with the even more negative future I saw for her. Eventually, I really had to repent for limiting God. I'm so glad God straightened out my thinking! I'm so glad I got into God's Word and now see things through His eyes. Now I see truth! The dictionary defines truth as the "highest reality," and God's reality is the highest reality. It's higher than any natural factor or diagnosis. Best yet, God's reality—His truth—can even change what we see in the natural.

These lessons have changed my life! Now at times I just sit and think about my very special Caroline in a whole new way. Through eyes of faith I see her completely healed, sitting having a cup of coffee with me as we share all the many good things God has done for us both.

See God in your children, in your family life and know that He knows no limits.

NINETY-NINE

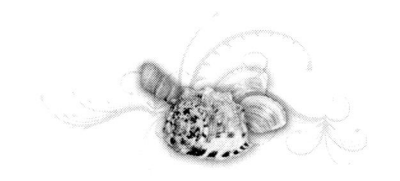

Mountain or Mole Hill

... IF YOU HAVE THE FAITH AS A MUSTARD SEED, YOU WILL SAY TO THIS MOUNTAIN, MOVE FROM HERE TO THERE, AND IT WILL MOVE; AND NOTHING WILL BE IMPOSSIBLE FOR YOU. —MATTHEW 17:20

Up until the 1960s it seemed that society went through a time of denying everything. Whether it was someone's alcoholism or abuse or sickness, people just stuffed their problems in a closet and tried to go on with their everyday life. The last thing most people wanted was for others to know their personal business and problems.

But that pendulum sure has swung. Lately it seems as though society fully embraces every problem by name and owns them with pride. There are reality TV shows left and right where people talk about things that should embarrass them. I'm embarrassed for them. Truly, we're now out of balance the other way. In fact, many people have become so diagnosed that they've begun to identify and align so closely with various diagnostic details that they are losing their own identity.

When Caroline was first born, it really bothered me when people referred to her as "that little Down's girl." I felt those words totally stripped her of individuality. Yes, most of us have mountains of one sort or another in our lives. But what did Jesus say to do about it? Sit and *talk about* our mountain or speak directly to it? Jesus didn't even say climb your mountain, and He sure didn't say spend the rest of your life *talking about* your mountain. No! He said to speak *to* it. Our job is to tell the mountain to leave and be gone, and with the measure of faith that Jesus gave each of us, this *is* possible.

The next verse goes on to say that with God all things are possible, and here's the really good news. If you're a Christian you're with God, which means there's no mountain too big to move. What looks like a big, old mountain is just a mole hill to God. With a little faith in Him, it will be blown away.

ONE HUNDRED

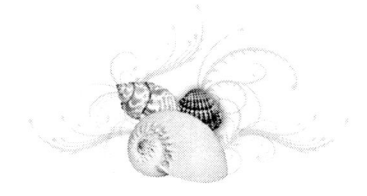

The Great Exchange

... TO GIVE THEM BEAUTY FOR ASHES.... —ISAIAH 61:3

I've seen kitchens on fire and houses that have almost burned. But in most cases even though there has been a fire that destroyed the outer parts of a room or house, you could still see what the room or the home looked like before it burned. On the other hand, if you come up on a pile of ashes, there's really no earthly way you can even guess what it was suppose to be. Once a fire has truly burned something up till only ashes are left, you can't tell what it was or what it was supposed to be.

This fact relates to life as well. When your life has been so burned that you or anyone else can't see what was or see any hope for restoration, then in your life you've reached a place of ashes. When a doctor tells a patient there is no hope and there is no changing the damage that has been done, people lose all hope. The despair and darkness that comes with that kind of reality is more than words can express. Only God in His Words can ever express exactly those kinds of feelings.

Isaiah 61 sums up the desperate state of mankind as God verbalized what mankind was going through and experiencing. Yet, notice that empathy was not all He offered. God offered something much better, declaring that He could completely change your life. He promised beauty for ashes.

When you think about it, only God could look at a pile of ashes and change it into something beautiful. You and I can't take a heap of ashes and create anything, much less something beautiful. And you and I as parents—no matter how much love we have—cannot change our child's life. But God can!

Our Father God, the ultimate parent, was moved by love to do what you and I could not do. He sent Jesus to do what no other could do. Jesus came to fulfill the law, and now all things are possible. So the next time you see that your life is void of any hope—you feel that situations are seemingly irreversible—know that God has promised to take what the fire left and make something beautiful out of it.

ONE HUNDRED & ONE

It Is Finished

... HE SAID, "IT IS FINISHED!" AND BOWING HIS HEAD, HE GAVE UP HIS SPIRIT. —JOHN 19:30

He who had no sin took on the sin of the whole world. He took forty stripes for every sickness that the devil could ever think up. He was betrayed by family and friends. He went all the way to Calvary knowing He had a way out. He was nailed to a Cross and died for the whole human race, and the veil was torn from top to bottom. He went to hell and conquered death and on the third day He rose again. Finally he left Earth blessing His followers and giving them all authority, and He sat down at the right hand of God.

It is finished. Everything we ever needed or think we might need has already been done. So now we need to stop running in circles and realize it is done. As we pursue our relationship with Him—through the Word and the Spirit—we more and more grow to understand all the amazing things accomplished when He said, "It is finished."

One year after teaching school for months, I'd say, "I really wish I had a large map hanging on the classroom wall. I'd love to teach the continents and pointing to a map would be so helpful for the children." I mentioned this several times even to my husband. Each time he'd say, "Why don't you buy one?" Then I'd go on to explain, "I've already spent all my school allowance." So the year would go on and from time to time it would enter my mind, but I'd dismiss it like it was something so out of reach.

Then one night near the end of school, I was cleaning and looked way in the back of a closet and to my amazement pulled out a large wall map. Even though it seems like a small thing, it made me realize that it was there every day I wanted it. Yet, I didn't know it. I had no idea something I wanted was so close.

That may seem like a small thing, yet there's a big point for us all. Some people are trying to figure out what they need; others know exactly what they need. No matter—God has all the answers and His Word says that He "hath already provided" everything we need that pertains to life and godliness. Wow, is that good news. Whether you need salvation, healing, direction, companionship—whatever—it's yours for the taking. Jesus said, "It is finished!" and all you need is closer than you could ever imagine. Don't go a lifetime in need! Take hold of everything He paid so dearly to give you.

An Opportunity to Pray with You!

Dear Reader and Friend,

Before you close the pages of this book, I want to give you an opportunity to make the most important decision of your life.

Throughout this book I've shared my experiences encouraging you to recognize the treasure in your own special circumstances. And yet, the greatest treasure you will ever find is in Jesus Christ Himself.

If you have not yet made Jesus Christ your Lord and Savior, I invite you to pray this prayer aloud now.

PRAYER OF SALVATION

Heavenly Father, Your Word says, "Whosoever shall call on the name of the Lord shall be saved" (Acts 2:21). I call on You right now. The Bible also says if I confess with my mouth that Jesus is Lord and believe in my heart that You have raised Him from the dead, I shall be saved (Romans 10:9-10). I make that choice now! I believe in my heart and confess with my mouth that You raised Jesus from the dead.

Jesus, I ask You to become my Lord and Savior. Please forgive me of all my sins. Thank You for it! I believe now that I'm a new creation in You. Old things have passed away; all things become new in Jesus' name (2 Corinthians 5:17). Amen.

If you've prayed this prayer, please share your good news with me at **www.tracybreland.com**.

About the Author

Author and special education teacher Tracy Breland shares a heart full of encouragement and a wealth of knowledge with parents in *Finding a Treasure: 101 Devotions for Parents of Special Children.*

Working to develop a special education program at Victory Christian School in Tulsa, Oklahoma, Tracy is degreed and certified in early childhood education, elementary education and special education. She brings many years of experience to her students.

Yet, perhaps her best preparation to author a devotional for parents comes from being not only a schoolteacher, but also the mother of five children and especially the mother of a daughter with Down syndrome.

Tracy attended Oral Roberts University and Southern Nazarene University, where she graduated with a bachelor's degree.

Now in addition to teaching, Tracy travels throughout the United States to inspire churches, groups and organizations with the truth that special children and special parents can live victoriously through the power of God's Word.

Tracy, her husband, John, and their children reside in Broken Arrow, Oklahoma.

For more information about Tracy or her book or to contact her as a speaker, visit **www.tracybreland.com**.

Dear Friend,

Now it's your turn!

Throughout these pages, I've shared my story with you. And now, I'd like to hear your story.

If you're the parent of child with special needs—or perhaps the grandparent, brother or sister or even special friend—then please write to share with me how God has worked in your life and helped you *find your treasure*.

I've prayed that these devotionals would minister encouragement to you so I would be very happy to hear from you directly. In fact, please visit me at www.tracybreland.com, and click on the "Share Your Treasure" link to tell me the story of how you found your treasure.

One special friend to another,

Tracy Breland

Share Your Treasure!

- ❧ Share how you found treasure walking through life with a special son or daughter, relative or friend.

- ❧ Share how God worked in your special circumstances.

- ❧ Share how God used this devotional to encourage you or a loved one to find your treasure.

  - ❧ Share your story at "Share Your Treasure" at **www.tracybreland.com.**

MAYBE YOUR STORY WILL BE INCLUDED IN TRACY'S NEXT BOOK!

Coming Soon!

A new children's book by Tracy Breland titled,
"Indy the Church Mouse"

Visit
www.tracybreland.com
or
www.mountzmedia.com
for more information on one adventurous little church mouse.

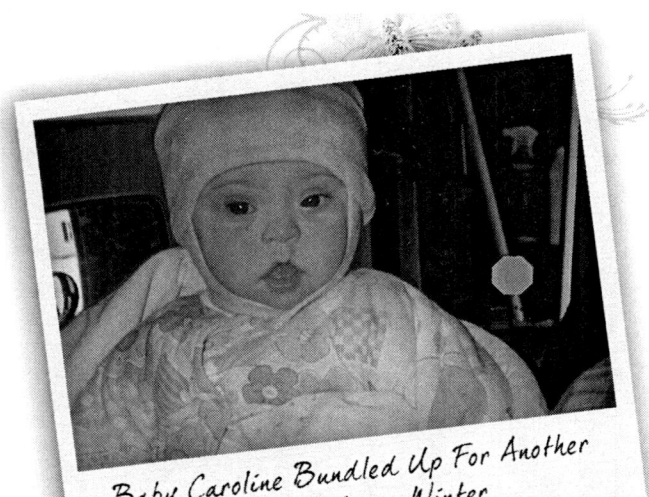

Baby Caroline Bundled Up For Another Cold Oklahoma Winter

Caroline, David, Elizabeth, John and Anna... Finally Dressed & Ready to Go Back to School

Nothing Like Having Fun With My Sister Anna

Our Beautiful Teenager Caroline

Another Wonderful Breland Family Vacation